TAR HEEL TRAVELER'S GOOD EATS

101 DOWN-HOME NORTH CAROLINA CLASSICS

D1286914

SCOTT MASON

Globe
Pequot

Guilford, Connecticut

Globe
Pequot

An imprint of The Rowman & Littlefield Publishing Group, Inc.
4501 Forbes Blvd., Ste. 200
Lanham, MD 2706
www.rowman.com

Distributed by NATIONAL BOOK NETWORK

British Library Cataloguing in Publication Information available

Library of Congress Control Number: 2019957602

ISBN 978-1-4930-4552-5 (paper : alk. paper)
ISBN 978-1-4930-4553-2 (electronic)

♾™ The paper used in this publication meets the minimum requirements of American National Standard for Information Sciences—Permanence of Paper for Printed Library Materials, ANSI/NISO Z39.48-1992.

PREFACE

MOM AND POP AND SWEETIE

I've heard of people putting books by the toilet.

You're welcome to do that with this one, but you may want to keep it in the car instead. Because you never know. You might find yourself on the road, belly growling with the engine, fast-food signs flitting past your window. But—*Nah, not another burger wrapped in paper. Fries in a box. Chicken in a box. Tacos in a bag. All the same.*

So, where to? You drum the wheel, peer at the painted line and wait for the next town. *"Maybe I'll find a cozy little Mom-and-Pop."* But mom-and-pops seem few and far between. If only . . .

Ah ha! I knew what you were thinking before you even thought it. Because I've been on the road, too, sat where you've sat, smeared ketchup on my khakis, gooped mayo on my Polo, spilled diet Coke in the console—it was flat, and not just the drink, but the whole kit and caboodle. Calories wasted on a drive-through. If only I had moseyed into some small town along the way where Mom and Pop were there to greet me and seat me and fill me with a homemade meal, while people chatted around me and even addressed me. "Howdy, fella."

And the waitress smiled at me, "Hey, sweetie, what can I getchya, shug?"

"Coffee, please."

There are places like that left in North Carolina. I know because I've seen them, sat in them, smiled back at the waitress, ordered biscuits and eggs, or burgers and dogs, or barbecue and hush puppies.

"Sure thing, hon. Be right back, shug."

"Take your time. No hurry."

And I mean it, the no hurry part. I believe I could sit all day and talk with the friendly people around me, salt-of-the-earth folks. Or sit and read the newspaper, and not from a screen, but one I crinkle and flip and that leaves ink on my fingertips. Or I could read a book. Or write a book, like the one you're reading now, pages inspired by the mom-and-pops I was blessed to visit along my travels.

All those wonderful travels . . . All one hundred North Carolina counties . . . I've seen them all, the beauty of being the Tar Heel Traveler. I roam the state, telling stories about people and places, history and landmarks. Which is what these down-home classics are: land-marks, each with their own history, places full of colorful people.

My Tar Heel Traveler series debuted in 2007 on WRAL-TV in Raleigh, and since then I've told more than two thousand Tar Heel Traveler stories. The features air four nights a week: Monday through Thursday at 5:55 p.m. and online at wral.com, and so, yes, that requires lots of content, week after week, year after year. Lots of travel, too.

The road stretches on, the engine drones, and the belly growls. And so this book, a restaurant guidebook; 101 down-home North Carolina classics—and the classics include a few high-end places as well. I visited them all, featured each one on TV. Ate at them, too—hey, I'm a reporter; depth is a necessary ingredient, which means plunging into every story. "Think I'll try some banana pudding."

"Sure thing, sweetie. Be right back, hon."

My *Good Eats* gives you a taste of these classics. Not a review or critique, no recipes or menus, but rather a flavor of what they are and how they came to be. I write about them through the lens of my experience: who I met, what I saw—what I ate! Oh, the meals I've had . . .

And yet the thing of it is, it's not really about the food. Well, sure, that's a big part of it, but in my eyes, it's about the places. Everybody should try them, skip the fast food drive-throughs and drive on to the next town in the book, stop at the little place on the corner, pull up a rickety chair or grab a wobbly stool at the counter. And please, say hello to Mom and Pop for me. Take your time, look around, enjoy the dish, absorb it all. Have fun, relax, be kind.

Fellow Tar Heel travelers may finish the book—thanks for reading it, by the way—and shout, "But wait! What about . . . ? He didn't include . . . ! Can't believe the knucklehead! He missed it! What the heck!?"

Maybe I should have made it 102 down-home classics, or 103, or . . . But isn't that encouraging, the fact that so many of these places still exist? In fact, I keep finding new ones myself—new old ones—on my many adventures. The floors creak, and the booths squeak—ah, my kind of places. Maybe the next edition . . . *201 Down-Home Classics!*

For now, enjoy the 101. Note the addresses and contact information at the beginning of each chapter, but also read what I pen, for it should help guide you to the gifts that wait. The comfy, cozy, delicious gifts that wait . . .

The rig rumbles and belly grumbles. You drum the wheel, peer past the window, looking, looking . . . The white lines skip, then turn double yellow, on and on.

But wait! There it is! On the passenger seat beside you. Or tucked in the glove box. Or thudding about the trunk next to the spare. The restaurant guide! *Tar Heel Traveler's Good Eats*. So many marvelously good eats. *101 Down-Home North Carolina Classics*.

Enjoy the journey. Cherish each and every one.

"Warm your coffee, sweetie?"

"Oh, yes, ma'am. Thank you."

"Back in a jiffy. Sit as long as you like, hon. Glad to have you, shug."

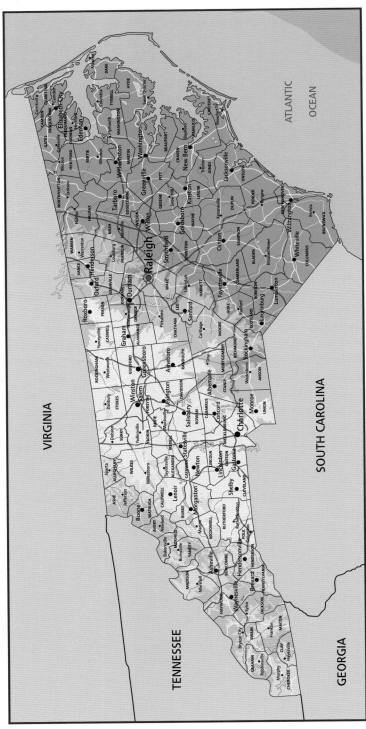

HOW TO USE THIS BOOK

I divide my book into three sections: Central, East, and West.

I begin with Central because that's where I live and work. In fact, I use WRAL-TV as my central starting point, as I did on my travels to all the restaurants that follow. The photographer and I—Robert is his name—hopped in the car, and away we went. Central starts with restaurants closest to WRAL, then fans out farther and wider.

I take a similar approach with the other sections, but use different starting points. Interstate 95 is my margin, dividing Central from East, and Interstates 85 and 29 form the border between Central and West—well, more or less. I begin the East and West sections at those lines. Then off I go, restaurant after restaurant, mile after mile, meal after meal.

Wow, that's a lot of meals. Three sections, 101 total restaurants. Time to diet.

Or, maybe not yet . . .

Maybe I should get to work on the sequel. The next one hundred and one!

If you've set out to visit every restaurant in a certain section of the book, in the order in which they're listed, you might find yourself happily driving from one to another in a reasonably straight line. But then—Whoa!—suddenly, the next restaurant, the next chapter, takes you in a whole different direction. It's by necessity, for there isn't a single direct and logical route that encompasses every Mom and Pop. Sometimes you have to veer. Sometimes radically.

It's tough mapping a guide book, there's no easy way. So here's what I suggest: Rather than gobbling an entire section in one bite, do it in nibbles. Focus on small sections within the bigger section. You might find that easier on the stomach anyway.

Now, you ready to go? Appetite packed? Guidebook handy?

Let's hit the road and enjoy some good eats!

—Scott Mason

CENTRAL

Aberdeen
Granny's Donuts, 54

Angier
Sunni Sky's Homemade
   Ice Cream, 28

Benson
Redneck BBQ Lab, 40
Big Steve's Bagels, 42

Burlington
Zack's Hot Dogs, 72

Carthage
Pik-n-Pig, 56

Cary
LaFarm Bakery, 22

Chapel Hill
Merritt's Grill, 64
Mama Dip's Kitchen, 66
Al's Burger Shack, 68
Ye Olde Waffle Shoppe, 70

Clayton
Jones Cafe, 34
The Grocery Bag, 36
Charlie's BBQ & Grille, 38

Dunn
Broad Street Deli & Market, 50
Sherry's Bakery, 52

Ellerbe
The Berry Patch, 83

Eure
Tarheel Bar-B-Q, 93

Franklinton
City Lunch Cafe, 32

Garland
Southern Smoke BBQ, 74

Laurel Hill
Mamie's Drive In, 81

Laurinburg
General McArthur's, 78

Littleton
Grandpa's Kitchen, 89

Milton
Aunt Millie's Pizza
   Subs & Suds, 91

Mt. Gilead
Lefler's Place, 76

Nashville
Doug Sauls BBQ and
   Seafood, 48

Raleigh
Cloos' Coney Island, 4
Amedeo's Italian Restaurant, 6
The Roast Grill, 8
Clyde Cooper's Barbecue, 10
Vic's Ristorante Italiano, 12
Circus Family Restaurant, 16
Ole Time Barbecue, 18
New York Bagels & Deli
   Raleigh, 20

Roanoke Rapids
Second Street Lunch, 85

CLOOS' CONEY ISLAND

2233-102 AVENT FERRY RD., RALEIGH, NC 27606, (919) 834-3354

People come for the ice. Crushed ice.

Of course they also come for the Coney Islands, hot dogs that travel all the way from Michigan. VIVA LA DETROIT! shouts a sign at the entrance. The mustachioed man behind the counter sports a Detroit Tigers T-shirt and waves when he sees me.

"Hello, Tar Heel Traveler!"

I've come to know Dan Cloos. His place is just a parking lot away from the TV station, and for somebody like me who loves to eat at moms-and-pops, and writes about eating, well, it's as if the Stanley Cup is in the backyard—brimming with crushed ice.

The walls celebrate hockey, especially that '06 moment when the Carolina Hurricanes won it all. I never tire of seeing the picture of team captain Rod Brind'Amour hoisting the cup, his sweaty face twisted in a scream both agonizing and exhilarating. The headline says it all: It's Ours!

Dan is from Hockeytown, and so are his hot dogs. "I drive to the airport myself and pick them up," he says. He's driven miles and cooked decades since opening Cloos' in 1988. "I'm actually more of a North Carolinian now than a Michigander," he says over his shoulder. He's tending the grill, which is sizzling with dogs, burgers, clumps of chicken, and shreds of steak. Phillys and pitas are on the menu, plus gyros, Reubens, subs, salads . . .

"Best french fries in town," belts a man with two crispy ones between his fingers. "Great!" He's got to holler over the lunch rush, though he's probably used to hollering. He's wearing an NC State shirt and stealing glances at the TV in the corner, which is tuned to ESPN.

"There is more girl talk than sports talk at our table," a sassy woman with dangly earrings tells me, swishing in her seat. She's just playing, and I love it. I've found the table in back marked RESERVED FOR CLOOS' CLUB, and today the Cloos' Club is five female members strong. "We talk about everything. I mean, this is like our therapy. Every-thing!" she says, rolling her eyes as giggles ripple all around.

The Cloos' clubbers are grown women, a decade or so older than I am, and this is obviously their go-to. "I'm a Friday only," the brunette

says. "But they are *evvverrry* day." She points a well-manicured finger at the others who collectively cringe with apparent embarrassment.

But they're giddy in their guilt. "I mean, we get more news per calorie than anywhere you could go!" pipes the frosted blonde. "And the owner is *soooo* good looking," she says loud enough for Dan to hear. He turns and gives them a wave with his spatula.

Just another day at Cloos'—on RED WINGS DRIVE reads a license plate nailed over a booth. Or is it WOLFPACK AVE?

"We love what we do," Dan says. He's still got the Michigan accent. And still has the spatula in hand. He punches the air for emphasis, and I worry about something dripping on his Tigers T-shirt, even though I'm a Red Sox fan. But that's the thing at Cloos': Everybody seems united—by the food, fellowship, and crushed ice. It's Ours!

"These people are my family," Dan says. The spatula doesn't drip. "We're all very lucky."

AMEDEO'S ITALIAN RESTAURANT

3905 WESTERN BLVD., RALEIGH, NC 27606, (919) 851-0473, AMEDEOSRESTAURANT.COM

The man holds up his hand.

"If this is a map of Italy," he says and shows me his palm, "and if this is Rome"—Rome is just below one of his calluses—"well, then this is where my ancestors lived." His Italian ancestors settled around his little finger.

Amedeo Deangelis is tall and bearded; his beard is white, his hands are big, and apparently, so were the dreams of his ancestors, many of whom found their way to the land of opportunity.

"What did you think about opening a restaurant?" I ask him.

"I didn't know what in the world I was doing," he admits—the man is blunt.

He opened Amedeo's Italian Restaurant in 1963 on Western Boulevard in Raleigh, just down the street from WRAL and close to NC State. It's a colorful, though dimly lit place, cozy in a box-like way. And maze-like, too, with rooms shooting off in different directions.

"This is the basketball room," Amedeo says and points to walls littered with NC State photographs, including those of the '83 men's championship team. In one photo Coach Jim Valvano is frozen in mid-air, snipping one of the last threads of the basketball net. Turns out, Valvano was one of the restaurant's regulars. "He ate his butt off here," Amedeo says—yep, blunt indeed.

He points to other recognizable faces, Wolfpack heroes, who in their day were regulars, too.

And then there's the Wolfpack player turned restaurant owner. We've come to the football wall, and I must say big number 73 doesn't look anything like the man leading me on the tour, but then the stud in the picture is a half-century younger and beard-free. "That's *you*?" I blurt, too late to take it back. But Amedeo doesn't seem offended; in fact, just the opposite.

He taps his old self on the shoulder pads. "No losses in 1957." His undefeated team won the Atlantic Coast Conference that year.

"I can name them all," he says as we walk past other walls plastered with pictures. "Of course, we got Roman," and I know exactly

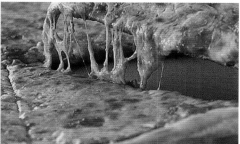

who he's talking about. I remember watching Roman Gabriel as a kid, quarterbacking for the NFL Rams, and rooted for him because I thought he had a cool name. But first, he became a star at NC State.

"Kay Yow," Amedeo says, and of course I also know her. The former Wolfpack women's basketball coach is from a more recent era and I remember her long struggle with cancer and eventual death. "Kay loved my mother's cheesecake," says Amedeo.

Amedeo's mother used to work at the restaurant; his children and grandchildren have pitched in as well. He tells me the food's good, always has been, and that he learned a lot from his Italian dad who ran a market in Philadelphia. The biggest picture is the grainy one by the front door. It's Amedeo just a few years old, a shrimpy little kid sitting with his dad in front of the market, and once again I nearly blurt, *"That's you?"*

The tour has me hungry, and so do the smells of tomato sauce and garlic. The restaurant's big seller is lasagna, a customer favorite—that, and the pizza. Right now, I think I could eat a whole pepperoni pie.

"I can understand why you love it," I say. "Even though you don't own it anymore." It's the hard, sad truth—the blunt reality. Amedeo nods and explains the deal. He sold the restaurant shortly before its fiftieth year but is quick to say he remains a partner, no longer at the restaurant every day but still a teammate, cheering from the sidelines.

"We're part of the Wolfpack family," he says and straightens, chest out. "And it makes me feel good, makes me feel real good."

I bet Amedeo's ancestors feel good, too, the ones nestled up there by his little finger. I bet they're proud of big number 73 and his success in the land of opportunity.

THE ROAST GRILL

**7 S. WEST ST., RALEIGH, NC 27603, (919) 832-8292,
ROASTGRILL.COM**

His name is George. But not just George. Hot Dog George.

The hot dogs are grilled. But not just grilled, burned.

"Black burned, medium burned, light burned," he growls and says I can order no burn if I'd like, but his bushy mustache turns down at the corners. No worries. I'm a black-burned man, the crispier the better, and tell him two all the way.

"No ketchup," he warns and aims his spatula like a poisoned arrow at the Heinz bottle on the shelf, the one with a big red X stamped

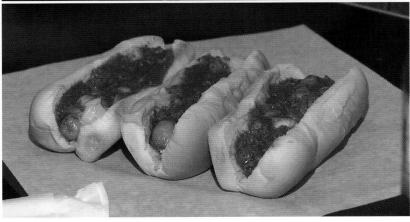

across the label. "Ketchup does not belong on a good hot dog." I shrug; no problem. I'm a mustard man; in fact, I tell him extra mustard.

It's a pale green shack of a place, with a neon sign in the window that reads, OPEN. The restaurant is four blocks west of the Capitol building—though I can't imagine the governor, in his double-breasted suit, lunches at the Roast Grill.

I'm wrong. Governors and plumbers have both rattled the front door—and probably waited for a place to sit. It's a shotgun shack, narrow, with a long counter to the right and tables lining the left, tables only for two and only a few.

The counter is elbow-to-elbow and Hot Dog George and his mom are just three feet away on the other side. Mom is busy popping tops off Coke bottles, the old-timey kind with ridges around the glass. Her hair is gray, skin dark, and arms long and thin but surprisingly strong—some of those tops aren't easy to twist.

"They came from Greece, Ellis Island, in the twenties," Hot Dog George says and points to a picture on the wall above the grill. It's of another gray-haired woman, dark skinned as well, her arms outstretched, and I can almost hear her say, *Welcome, welcome!"* in broken English but with genuine joy.

"Keep it simple," Hot Dog George says. "That's rule number one, and Grandma made the rules." His eyes fall from Grandma to me. "Rule number two is don't change the rules."

The Roast Grill has been roasting dogs since 1940, all that time under the same family. "And one of the things Grandma left me with was try and continue to keep this place making hot dogs." His bushy mustache turns up at the corner.

"He knows when you walk in the door exactly how you want them," a lady at the counter tells me. She looks rather fashionable in a blue dress and straw hat, especially compared to the man clad in gray sitting next to her, his shirtsleeves tightly rolled above his biceps and three dogs "all the way" in front of him—make that two-and-a-half all the way; he's begun to chow.

Somebody else orders six to go, chili only, and Hot Dog George adds another pile to the grill. His mom grabs more Cokes from the cooler. Grandma looks down from the wall.

I can practically hear Grandma now: *Welcome, welcome!*

CLYDE COOPER'S BARBECUE

327 S. WILMINGTON ST., RALEIGH, NC 27601, (919) 832-7614, CLYDECOOPERSBBQ.COM

You must taste the meat first. The meat, not the sauce. The sauce is just the kiss on the meat.

That was Clyde Cooper's mantra, though I doubt he would have used the word *mantra*—too fancy.

"Clyde Cooper was my very good friend," says an old-timer, loud enough for half the room to hear. "I'm ninety-three and come here almost every Saturday." *Ninety-three?* I think. The man seems mighty spry for his age, though he is the only one in the place wearing a necktie while eating barbecue.

He tells me Clyde was just a good ol' fella, down-to-earth and folksy. "And most of all, he enjoyed ringing that cash register," he says and slaps the table. I worry about the sauce on his plate splattering his tie. Though I don't think he gives it a thought because of the—mantra. Clyde's been dead a long time, and I never met the man but imagine him saying something like, "*Sauce? Why you frettin' over that? Sauce ain't the thing. It's the meat!*"

SLAP! The old-timer jars me and the table—and the sauce again. At ninety-three he still packs a punch. "Eastern-North-Carolina style," he says, as though it's the only style of barbecue on God's green earth. "And you cannot beat it."

To me, Clyde Cooper's Barbecue oozes nostalgia: all the old pictures crowding the walls, a classic lunch counter with a line of stools, lots of chrome, and plenty of people—working folks, hungry folks bent over plates, and waitresses asking if everything's okay, then fetching pitchers to top off sweet teas, stopping only to pull pencils from behind their ears and scribble more orders. Plus, the whole place seems to be coated in a sepia-tone tint, and I somehow suspect Clyde Cooper wanted it that way. Okay, okay, so the meat's the thing. But the atmosphere counts for something, too.

"Evidently, the man was doing something right because it's been here for more than seventy-five years. So, yeah, you don't mess with what's not broken," says Debbie Holt while punching at the register. Debbie owns Clyde Cooper's Barbecue with her husband, Randy.

"It's just slow cooked all night long," Randy says, lifting the lid off a wide grill. Smoke billows, then clears, revealing long slabs of roasted meat that appear cooked to perfection, no ifs, ands, or—butts. Shoulders only. "Nice and moist," Randy says, and I'm thinking Clyde Cooper would surely approve of Randy's work. And he'd probably carve a juicy hunk for himself to sample.

Clyde opened the place in 1938 in downtown Raleigh. "It's the same table, chairs, same pictures on the walls," Debbie says. "People come in here, and they just love the oldness of it."

"It's an institution!" belts the tie-wearing old-timer, except this time he doesn't slap the table; his hands are busy with his meal. He's in the middle of his barbecue, and I must say, it looks pretty saucy, and he might have to throw his tie in the wash when he gets home. But that's okay, because in the words of Clyde Cooper, the sauce is merely the kiss. The meat's the thing.

The meat is what ties it all together.

VIC'S RISTORANTE ITALIANO

331 BLAKE ST., RALEIGH, NC 27601, (919) 646-8167, VICSRISTORANTEITALIANO.CLUB

I have a conflict of interest.

My son has worked as a busboy at Vic's since he was fourteen. Now he's seventeen and has eaten more pasta than I have in my lifetime—he gets a discount.

"The pasta, veal, chicken, seafood, everything," says Mario Longo in a tongue thick with Italian flavor; I can barely understand him. But I *do* understand him. It helps that he waves his hands when he talks.

"I guess it's authentic Italian," I say.

"That's it. You got it. You got it."

Mario owns Vic's Ristorante Italiano; the name rolls of his tongue—and off mine, too. I exaggerate the accent and can't wait to dig in to some honest-to-goodness Italian. Despite the discount, my son rarely brings me home a dish.

Even the cook is Italian. I ask if he minds me looking over his shoulder, and he mutters something and shrugs—good enough for me—and goes about swishing pasta in a pan. Then he squirts something in, and—POW! Fire erupts. Flames shoot two feet high, and I jump three feet back. But the conflagration soon dies. Impressive. Authentic. It must be—I'm convinced Italians have a flair for the dramatic.

"No English at all, no job," Mario says.

It's 5 p.m., just before the dinner rush, and we're sitting near one of the big front windows with a view of Moore's Square, which is that quaint little pocket in downtown Raleigh: cobblestone streets and twinkly lights, other cozy restaurants with outdoor seating, red-wine glasses on iron tables, and an occasional twirl of cigarette smoke wafting toward the dusky sky.

"No English?" I say.

He shrugs, spreads his arms, waves his hands, and then picks up the menu and flips it over and shows me the familiar picture of Italy. "Italy, south Italy," he says and points and names the town where he grew up, which is *un*familiar to me and rather garbled. So I boil it down—all the way down.

"You're from the toe of the boot."

"Right, right, right," he says. "You got it, you got it."

He tells me he journeyed to America at age fifteen and settled in New York. "I started working, like a dishwash." In time, he went from dishwasher to restaurant owner and from New York to North Carolina.

"So you started in Cary, North Carolina?"

"In Cary, yeah, at the mall. Cousins Pizza."

He shows me the Cousins logo, the sketch of a mustachioed man wearing a tall chef's hat and holding a pizza pie. I peer closely. He looks like Chef Boyardee—or maybe a cousin.

"And then I start to open more restaurants, more restaurants with a different name." He tells me he opened twenty different restaurants in North Carolina.

"Twenty restaurants?" I say. *And could barely speak English?* I think.

"Yeah," he says and shrugs, waves his hands and laughs.

He then heard about a restaurant in Moore's Square. "Nighttime it was nothing," he says. The cobblestone streets were all but deserted, but he bought the place anyway, bought it from Vic in 1993 and left the name but changed the menu: authentic Italian, and slowly but surely people followed. Other restaurants and businesses did, too. "And Moore's Square went up, up," Mario says. "So I must have do something right."

Or three things right, anyway. His three kids work alongside him. Michael is the pizza maker. "We make our own sauce, our own dough."

Mia is a waitress. "The food is amazing. Reminds me of childhood, because that's what we had growing up."

And then there's Mario, Jr. who today runs his own Vic's at a second Raleigh location, following in his dad's footsteps. "He's a great role model. You know, to come here with nothing . . . " Actually, Junior's footsteps are much faster; he used to play professional soccer. "He gave me the opportunity. Yeah, when he was working here, I was playing on the TV there."

The TV sits on a shelf, tuned to a soccer game; the announcers are British, and the action is back and forth. The walls are more interesting: elaborately painted murals of scenic Italy. There's also a portrait of Mario, Sr., puffing a fat cigar, and I must say, the artist captured him perfectly, right down to the gleam in his eye. "Authentic Italian," I say more to myself than to him.

But he hears me and spreads his arms, waves his hands, and laughs. "That's it. You got it, you got it."

CIRCUS FAMILY RESTAURANT

1600 WAKE FOREST RD., RALEIGH, NC 27604, (919) 834-2213

It sits by itself at Wake Forest Road and Capital Boulevard in Raleigh, its own little island at a busy intersection. Traffic is a circus—and the restaurant is, too.

The Circus Family Restaurant opened in the 1950s. Before that, it was a Dairy Queen with a dirt parking lot, though nowadays that may be hard for people to picture, for the Circus has become an icon with its red-and-yellow awning and green top.

"I started working here in high school in the mid-eighties," says Glenn Mitchell who today is the proud owner—the ringmaster. "We make the food the same way we did when I started here."

The menu lists burgers and fries and hot dogs and shakes, and people order at the window and take it to go or sit in the side room. "A lot of people know about this place," says a man in a wooden booth with a cheesesteak. "They go, 'Oh, yeah, the Circus Restaurant.'"

Another man seated nearby is bending his ear to my interview and chimes in. "Gives me so many memories of my teenage years," he says and talks at length about the good old days.

The walls are full of good old Thanksgiving days. For years, the Circus has served a free Thanksgiving meal, open to anyone: the rich, the homeless, the jobless, the hungry—although I'm sure everybody's hungry by the mounds of turkey and sweet potatoes at the center of

the snapshots. Volunteers supply much of the food, churches pitch in, and it's a huge feast; the pictures are full of grins and hugs. "There's lots of sad stories, but by the time they leave they have a smile on their face," Glenn says.

An especially sad story is the one about Leroy Jernigan, a Circus employee shot to death during a robbery at the restaurant in 2006. He was a husband and father of two. "The kind of guy who would do anything for you," Glenn tells me. "He would let strangers live in his attic." The Thanksgiving meal is in honor of Leroy. "It's my favorite day of the year."

"I bet Leroy is smiling," I say.

Glenn looks up, a moment of contemplation beneath the big top. "He is," the ringmaster announces. "He is."

OLE TIME BARBECUE

6309 HILLSBOROUGH ST., RALEIGH, NC 27606, (919) 859-2544

Jessica and Eden, Tommy and Allen, Vickie and Ken, Don and Toot—all longtime regulars at Ole Time Barbecue in Raleigh.

They eat so often at Ole Time their names are inked on the wall with a red Sharpie. "The people we've befriended over the years is just priceless," says owner Jerry Hart. He's a big man in a black T-shirt with a motorcycle parked out front who talks with a raspy voice, rough and hoarse—maybe from calling out so many orders over the years.

He opened his place in 1993, a long, narrow, yellow building near the Raleigh-Cary line, crammed with tables and a counter, that's known for barbecue and breakfast. "Oh, we got a killer breakfast," says Jerry's son, Ben, another big man, who runs the day-to-day. "And I killed three people last week."

I laugh, but he doesn't; he's too busy. It's lunchtime, and there's not a seat to be had. Customers talk up the homemade 'cue, the mac and cheese, collards, and fried okra. "Food and fellowship," says an older gentleman patiently waiting for his meal, and when he tells me his name is Don, I ask if he's *the* Don, the one on the wall in red Sharpie. He responds with a sheepish nod, and I can't believe my good fortune, a great element for my story; when we put it together, we'll be able to edit from the name to the person. Although I can't help it, I'm greedy and wish we'd met the owner of another Sharpie name: Toot. It's catchy and would have been *sensational* for my story.

Jerry collars me again and steers me to a big billboard with crinkled pictures of happy customers, some who've moved away, a few who've passed away. "They're remembered," he says, in a voice softer than before.

The snapshots include Ole Time regulars who are soldiers, clad in fatigues and posing in the field, some even holding OTB stickers and smiling. I guess they thought enough of Ole Time to mail Jerry their photos. "Some are deployed right now," he says. "They've got to come home and let us know they're back safe." His eyes slide from picture to picture, face to face. When they do make it back, he says, they get to sign their names on the wall.

ALL ARE FRIENDS WHO ENTER HERE. That slogan is on the wall, too, up high where everyone can read it as soon as they enter.

"The first time you come in and eat with us, you're our customer," Jerry says, his raspy voice nicked with emotion. "After that, you're our family."

NEW YORK BAGELS & DELI RALEIGH

7909 FALLS OF NEUSE RD., RALEIGH, NC 27615, (919) 848-1310, NYBAGELRALEIGH.COM

I don't dare wear my Boston Red Sox hat.

Although on my visits to the bagel shop in north Raleigh, I've actually become rather used to the New York Yankees, to seeing sluggers in pinstripes posing between picture frames. I've even been tempted to toast Derek Jeter with my coffee, thankful he's retired and will no longer pester my beloved team.

The New York City skyline is spread across an entire wall, and that's okay, too. It gives the place a Yankee authenticity. You just know the food is going to be good—not just any old bagels, but New York bagels. In New York, everything is bigger and better, or so they say.

I order a rye bagel, toasted, with pastrami, egg, and cheese, and how many places in Raleigh offer pastrami? Or even rye? How many bagel shops toast the bagels on a grill? That's the way it's done at New York Bagels & Deli, at least twenty-five different bagels to choose from, and everything made to order.

Bob Nurrito is the owner, and he works the wee hours of the morning, rolling dough. How many bagel shops make their own

bagels? "Takes a little longer," Bob says, "but they come out better, stay softer."

Bob's father and grandfather were bakers; his dad came over from Italy, and for years the family ran a bakery in New Jersey. But then Bob and his wife decided to move south because of better climate and lower taxes. Plus, Southerners like bagels and baseball, too. "And we really found that we liked the area," says Bob's wife, Joann.

"I knew we'd be a success," adds his daughter, Gabby, who works the counter wearing a Yankees ball cap. "I knew my dad's food." And it's obvious she knows her family's team.

The food includes breakfast and lunch and, on game days, subs taller than my teenage son who's nearing six feet. It takes three staff members to maneuver one out the door to the station-wagon-sized car that delivers them.

My son loves the deli's double-chocolate muffin, and it's tough passing up the crumb cake with my coffee. The desserts and danish are all made from scratch.

Even the staff is sweet, the Manhattan skyline spread across their T-shirts, northern accents heavy on their tongues.

"Sometimes I don't understand what they're saying," says a well-dressed woman sipping coffee. "But that's okay." She's with several chatty couples squeezed around two tables—her church group, she says, and tells me she's a native North Carolinian who appreciates the deli's hospitality. As do her fellow parishioners who insist the bagels are actually better than ones they've tried on trips to New York.

I hear, "Y'all, it's the God's honest truth" at the table.

I also hear, "Amen."

"Once you get down here, you love it," says Bob's son, Rob, who also works at the restaurant and says he doesn't miss New York at all. "I won't go back."

"You won't?" I ask and press him a bit because, after all, it's New York, the Big Apple, the bright lights. The deli even celebrates the city with a sub called the New Yorker, piled high with five different meats. In New York, everything's big.

Rob backpedals. "Well, yeah," he admits and hangs his head a bit. Maybe he will go back, he says. Maybe to see a Yankees game.

LAFARM BAKERY

4248 NW CARY PKWY., CARY, NC 27513, (919) 657-0657, LAFARMBAKERY.COM

"New customers come in, we give them a sample of our bread, and they're speechless."

The bread is French. And at times, so is the speech. "Tre bon," I say when the chef hands me a piece fresh from the oven, one much larger than my French vocabulary. But, when in France . . .

The chef is Lionel Vatinet. "We bring everything together," he says in his heavy accent. He works the dough, palms it, rolls it, sprinkles it, brings the ingredients together. Just as he brings people together. His French bakery in Cary stays constantly busy. There's a sizeable eating area and full menu. But, of course, the accent is on bread.

Such fresh bread . . . that warm and delicious aroma . . . and so many varieties. He offers me another piece, this one with white chocolate inside. "Merci beaucoup," I say, and he smiles. I think he appreciates the manners and my attempt at his native tongue.

He grew up near Paris, joined a famed artisan baking guild at age sixteen, and for years studied with some of Europe's best bakers. But perhaps his greatest achievement came at a trade show in the states when a random attendee sampled his ciabatta and fell immediately in love. "I was addicted," she exclaims. "I said, 'Who made this?'" Her future husband did, that's who.

Missy and I sit at a table amid the lunch hubbub. LaFarm Bakery is her bakery, too, hers and Lionel's. She's a ponytailed blonde who grew up in Virginia. "Did you ever think you'd marry a Frenchman?"

"Not at all," she says and laughs.

Missy and Lionel dreamed of starting their own bakery. "We actually looked all over the country for a location," she tells me. They apparently made the right decision when they opened LaFarm on Cary Parkway in 1999. "We haven't looked back. We have the most incredible customer base."

Lionel agrees. "Our customers . . . incredible," he says.

The ovens in back are enormous, and Lionel seems to know exactly when to pull the loaves out, no timer needed. Then there's the *way* he pulls them out. He slides a long-handled board, a kind of oversized paddle, beneath a hot loaf and pulls it swiftly and shows me, displaying the bread as he would an ornate work of art. Indeed, he seems both baker *and* artist.

Lionel has won prestigious James Beard cooking awards, and I admire copies of his book at the cafe, a beautiful hardcover called *A Passion for Bread*. Which begs my next question. "Si vou plais," I begin, "after all these years, do you still have the passion, the . . . amour?"

Lionel smiles again. I think he appreciates the interest—and the French. "I love it," he says—the accent on *love*.

SHORTY'S FAMOUS HOT DOGS

214 S. WHITE ST., WAKE FOREST, NC 27587, (919) 556-8026

If somebody mentions Wake Forest, I always think of Shorty's.

"You're from Wake Forest?" I ask. "Been to Shorty's?"

"Oh, all the time." I think they think of Shorty's, too.

It's the oldest restaurant in Wake Forest. Since 1916. "We been around a while," says owner Chris Joyner who runs the register. "Cheeseburger, chili cheese, fry, hot dog and a tea." He also calls out orders to the cook.

"I been coming here since 1942," a man at the counter tells me.

"Since '42?" I ask. "Well, that's over seventy years."

"I think it's a pretty good place myself."

"Well, I guess so," I say and chuckle at his "pretty good" understatement.

The place itself is understated, simple, not a big place but always packed, and where the plumber and lawyer sit elbow-to-elbow, a place even the famous have been known to frequent.

A picture of the late Arnold Palmer is on the wall. He's driving a ball off a tee, presumably driving it straight. Chris tells me the golfer used to drive straight to Shorty's whenever he was nearby. "Had his eightieth birthday party here back in '03, I think."

Palmer knew about Shorty's from his days as an undergrad at what was then Wake Forest College. So did actor Carroll O'Connor. They were both students before the college left town, moved to Winston-Salem, and became a university.

O'Conner won four Emmys for his role in the 1970 TV sitcom *All in the Family*. A decade later, he played a Mississippi sheriff in the crime drama *In the Heat of the Night*—a sheriff with a southern drawl. Apparently, the accent came easy to him; he picked it up from his time at Shorty's shooting nine ball, so the story goes.

Shorty's started as a pool room and only later became known for its hot dogs. "I like the soft buns," a lady tells me. "And the fact the hot dogs are grilled rather than boiled." She picks one up and shows me, though it's hard to get a look beneath all that chili. "Hmm," she murmurs. "I'm just in love with this place."

I can actually feel the love myself. I see people enjoying their lunch and each other and sense a timeless energy within the yellowy walls. It's a good feeling—and a full feeling after eating two all the way and going back for a third. I can't help it, and I bet Arnold and Carroll couldn't either. When I think of Wake Forest, I also think of them.

I clean the plate, or rather the wax paper, and waddle for the door, and when I do, a sign catches my eye. I reach for my pad, albeit with some effort—naptime is calling. I manage to copy down the line because I'm certain I'll use it in my script. It just feels right—and so did the hot dogs.

TIMES CHANGE BUT SHORTY'S STAYS THE SAME.

AUBREYS AND PEEDIES GRILL

38 N. MAIN ST., WENDELL, NC 27591, (919) 365-5528

BLT sandwich: $4.00; hamburger: $3.00; grilled cheese: $2.00. The numbers are round, and so is the table.

It's just inside the front door, and all eight or ten seats are taken and have been for an hour or three or four. It's a men's group, obvious retirees. It's mid-morning and nobody's in a hurry to scoot. Instead they lean on their elbows and play with their half-empty mugs, slide them between their calloused hands; the coffee sloshes but doesn't spill. They crack smiles and jokes and grumble a little, too, especially at news they don't favor. What do them dern politicians know anyhow? Leave it to the table to straighten things out. The Table of Knowledge at Aubreys and Peedies.

"I been coming here forty-nine years," growls one of the old-timers, but I can tell it's a good-natured growl because it quickly slips into a chuckle when his buddy next to him pipes up.

"Well, we talk about each other a lot." Now the whole table busts out laughing, and I wonder if the caffeine has made them giddy. "You learn all the gossip in town."

True, but in time I also learn some good history from the table. I learn Aubrey Edwards bought the grill in 1979. "Aubrey kept things simple," somebody says, and heads nod all around. "Simple so it wasn't debatable."

One of the nodders points to the menu board on the wall above the grill. "That's what you pay is $3.00. It's not $3.00 plus tax, or $3.00 plus this. It's just $3.00."

My eyes roam the board. *Hmm*. The egg plate with country ham, grits and biscuits sounds tempting: $7.00 even. And I could sure use some coffee if the Table of Knowledge hasn't drained it all.

"I love 'em," says Aubrey's son, Peedie, who swings by to greet the men—and to tease them. "They may drink all my coffee, but I do love 'em." The table busts out laughing again.

I interview Peedie by the grill, because that's where he stands much of the time, cooking eggs and burgers and grilling chicken and fried bologna sandwiches. And carrying on what his dad began. "We're like one big family," he says.

Peedie is a tall fella. Me? I'm on the short side, and yet I detect puddles in his eyes. "My dad was in a car wreck February the fourth, 2010," he says. "And he died on February the thirteenth from complications."

The dates jog my mind: the fourth and thirteenth, one even, one odd. I bet Aubrey wouldn't have liked that; the numbers don't add up. The equation doesn't make sense. But what can you do?

I suppose you do what Peedie does. Keep the name on the door: Aubreys and Peedies. Keep the grill going and the coffee pot full—an effort with the Table of Knowledge. And keep some round numbers on the board. *Hmm*. The $4.00 BLT sounds good, too. Although I hear the place is known for biscuits.

Peedie introduces me to the biscuit lady who has worked at the grill for thirty years. She's surprisingly thin—too busy making them to eat them, I guess.

"Any idea how many biscuits you've made over the years?"

"Oh, Lordy," she cries and tosses her head back. "Millions! Billions!" I hate to ask but wonder if she wouldn't mind making one more. "Oh, Lordy!"

I get a kick out of seeing the biscuit lady shout at the ceiling. And it's funny hearing the old-timers laugh and grumble. It's tough solving the world's problems. Best to keep things simple—the way Aubrey did.

"Do you feel like his presence is still here?" I ask Peedie.

"It is," he says. "Everything we do, we always know Daddy's around."

SUNNI SKY'S HOMEMADE ICE CREAM

8617 NC-55, ANGIER, NC 27501, (919) 427-7118, SUNNISKYS.COM

Apple pie!

Yes, I do enjoy a big ol' appley slice. Please make it extra thick. And, pretty please, top it with a giant scoop of vanilla. Yes!

But wait . . . What's this? Whoa! The apple pie *is* the ice cream.

Sunni Sky's Homemade Ice Cream in Angier is full of surprises. And flavors. Tiramisu, Crumb Cake, Cake Batter . . . am I in a bakery? Strawberry Daiquiri, White Russian . . . or a bar? My eyes travel down the board, and my jaw drops lower with every name: Key Lime, Eggnog, Rum Raisin, Pink Grapefruit . . . What exactly is this place?

"Our own little mom-and-pop," says Scott Wilson. He's tall and trim and at the moment no doubt thankful for his lanky frame. He's bent over an enormous aluminum bowl, using his height to lend him the leverage he needs for stirring with a long spoon.

"What flavor's that?" I ask, leaning in for a peek.

"Strawberry cheesecake," he grunts. "My favorite."

The board by the counter lists more than a hundred flavors, 100 percent homemade, and everybody in the place—and outside the place, in the rockers on the front porch—are oohing and ahhing while licking and slurping.

"Cinnamonny and delicious," mumbles a young girl in ponytails, nibbling on a double scoop of Cake Batter. "Tastes just like vanilla birthday cake." I bet the Apple Pie tastes just like apple pie.

It's fun watching the porch sitters. The whole row rocks and licks at the same time.

"Love coming here."

"So many flavors."

"Wonderful. Amazing."

"Terrible. Nasty." Huh?

The whiskered dude in the white T-shirt corkscrews his face and smacks his lips and sputters something about a cold sweat. "Cold sweat?" I ask. Turns out, it's one of the flavors, and there's another called Exit Wound, both loaded with hot peppers, habaneros, and the like, spicy as all get out. "Hot," he sputters.

HOTTEST KNOWN PEPPERS, reads the sign. DANGEROUSLY HOT! So hot any-one willing to try them must sample Cold Sweat first—to make sure they don't keel over—and then sign a waiver to attempt Exit Wound.

"A waiver to eat ice cream?" I ask.

Scott grins. "Yeah, we've gotten a lot of attention for those." No wonder he's grinning; he's received nationwide publicity in the form of newspaper and magazine articles, and I figure the man must be a marketing genius.

He tells me he spent years in the restaurant business, bartending and waiting tables before taking a chance on ice cream with encouragement from his wife. "I think people probably laughed when we said we were going to start an ice cream shop in Angier."

The shop is on the outskirts of town, along a lonely stretch of Highway 55. "Our daughter is Sunni, spelled with an i, and our son is Skylar." And so he named the shop Sunni Sky's, opened the doors, and crossed his fingers. "It also came down to prayer," he says.

Prayer and marketing and living a little. I should probably do the same, maybe order Root Beer ice cream or some other wacky flavor. Coffee ice cream is my favorite but boring, I guess, given the selection. I settle on a happy medium. Mocha it is.

The rockers are full, but that's okay. It's a sunny afternoon—make that sunni—with a blue sky overhead, and the Mocha is creamy and delicious. I lick and slurp and ooh and ahh just like everybody else.

And it occurs to me Scott Wilson's prayer has been answered.

COUNTY LINE
GROCERY & GRILL

2981 PILOT-RILEY RD., ZEBULON, NC 27597, (919) 269-0024

It sits eight inches from the county line.

"We're in Franklin County, and this is Wake County," David Bunn says and points—and his finger might cross the line.

But the building he owns doesn't—though it comes awfully close. "We didn't want to get a building permit in two counties," he explains. So he built in Franklin County, eight inches from Wake, a measly eight inches—but a bunch of square feet. Four-thousand square feet.

The County Line Grocery & Grill is big for a convenience store, a crisp red-brick building built in 2012 in the Zebulon countryside. Zebulon is the easternmost town in Wake County, but a tiny portion sneaks into rural Franklin. A big store in a rural area? "Didn't know how it was going to work," David says. "I was scared to death."

He put in a grill at one end with a few tables and booths. "They make a good hamburger here," says a man in line with a weathered face and denim shirt. He might be a farmer, and I wonder if burgers are his usual. Although the menu is long and includes chicken wraps and Reubens, salads and taco salads, Philly cheesesteaks and fried pickles, lunch and breakfast.

"Everything's fresh, made to order," says one of the waitresses.

"And shrimp on Friday nights," says a man who tells me he's a Friday regular.

In addition to food, the store sells tools, plants, sleds, umbrellas, and American flags. The inside looks like a log cabin: lots of wood, ceiling fans, and nostalgic knickknacks. Old metal lunchboxes rest on a shelf, and lighted gas signs hang on the wall—a store with decorative touches. "The country feel with modern conveniences," David says.

He's in his forties, thin and fit with a heady determination about him, even though he grew up in the laid-back country. His boyhood home is just a few feet away, a brick ranch, and his granddaddy used to run a country store.

"You think that store got in your blood?" I ask.

"Must have."

David built *his* store on part of his granddad's land, then waited for customers to find it. "It was so slow when I opened, I'd get excited when a car came by."

Cars soon began stopping.

"The community has supported this place profoundly," David says, and he means people from both sides of the county line, though he's glad he made the choice he did. "Proud to be in Franklin County," he says.

"I wonder if the Wake County folks wish you'd come over there."

"They probably do now," he says and laughs. The laughter, I think, comes from both relief and success. He laughs hard enough that he bends at the waist—and I wonder if his head crosses the county line.

If so, it's only by a hair.

CITY LUNCH CAFE

5 S. MAIN ST., FRANKLINTON, NC 27525, (919) 494-5815,
CITYLUNCHCAFE.WIXSITE.COM/CLCAFE

I meet a man who could be the poster boy for North Carolina—born, bred, and proud of it.

He wears a John Deere hat and blue jean overalls, which I bet are extra-large—or extra-extra. There's little room between his belly and the table, maybe a quarter inch—might be less after lunch. "I got three hot dogs, two hamburgers, two french fries," he says, eyeing his plate, which the waitress sets in front of him—she uses two hands.

Speaking of his eyes, they're dancing, and, Jimminy Christmas, I've never seen eyes so agile. They're as big and round as his hamburger bun—I think he might have ordered the two-patty special.

He rests his tree-trunk-sized arms on either side of the dish, and his meaty fingers do their own little dance. "I'm gonna do something to it, you know what I mean?" he asks in a voice that could twang a banjo, his grin as thick as ketchup. But, uh oh, I distract him, as does the camera that's closing in, aiming for the money shot. He glances up, still grinning, tells me his name is Wilbur—but of course it is. "I always been big," he says, more to the camera than to me, "but I don't call it fat. I call it blessed with gravitational pull." He laughs so hard that poof goes the quarter inch, and his belly smooches the lip of the table. Then he picks up the burger with one huge hand, a hot dog with the other, and goes to town.

This is City Lunch where everybody seems to have a big appetite and sense of humor. Well, except for Sharon. She's the tall, skinny owner who growls by the grill. "Hamburger, put on a hamburger!" she belts, and the obedient cook snaps to attention and gets to work.

"Everybody's friendly," says a pleasant, soft-spoken man at the counter. But then the corners of his mouth droop, and his voice rises. "Except for Sharon!" Uh oh. Sharon whirls around, balls up a paper napkin and throws it at him, hitting him in the noggin. The man nearly falls off his stool, but I think it's because he's laughing so hard. Even Sharon cracks a smile, but only a crack—maybe a quarter inch.

"Don't believe nothin' they say!" she shrieks. "They're lyin'!"

But no, they aren't, not about their feelings for the place.

"Lot of camaraderie, lot of friendship, lot of love," says a transplant named Tony who's right off the streets of Manhattan. His accent

comes with a spicy bite, and yet he tells me how everybody welcomed him when he moved to Franklinton, especially the kind folks at City Lunch. "Well, except for Sharon," he whispers, though loud enough for her to hear, and I automatically flinch. Incoming! Although she's too occupied right now to reach for the paper cannonball.

"Another hamburger!" she shrieks to the cook.

Clyde is Sharon's opposite and, believe it or not, her partner. They're married, have been for years, and he's as laid back as an egg over easy; City Lunch serves breakfast, too. Clyde's mom and dad opened the restaurant in 1949. He describes them as good Christian folks, and he's carried on that tradition as well; the picture window bears an illustration of Jesus, head bowed in prayer. "It's just family," Clyde says, meaning both his immediate family and the customers.

Clyde and Sharon's daughter Michelle makes all the desserts. She shows me her chocolate cake and pecan pie, and I'm tempted while there's time—before she shows them to Wilbur.

"Gravitational pull!" he mumbles, his mouth full.

"Like one big happy family," several people tell me.

"Love it. Delicious." Several people say that, too.

"Hamburger!" Sharon shrieks. "Put on another hamburger!"

JONES CAFE

415 E. MAIN ST., CLAYTON, NC 27520, (919) 553-7528

I'm never quite sure what I'll find when I walk into a story. Especially a restaurant story.

Usually I walk in, all eyes gape at our enormous camera, and everybody backs away—that I can be sure of. *Whoa, not me! Don't point that thing over here!*

What happens next is up in the air. Will everyone remain camera shy, or will folks extract their backs from their booths and step up to the mic? If everyone remains camera shy, I'm sunk.

I felt as if I *was* sinking, standing inside the front door of what's now known as Jones Cafe (It was called Jones Lunch on my visit in 2010). I listed, shifted weight from one foot to the other, smiled weakly but groaned loudly. Otherwise, you could have heard a pin drop.

I'm not sure how long I floundered at the front door before Ann rescued me. She sat in the middle of the restaurant, at the end of a long table, and hoisted her arm high and waved her hand: *This way, young fella.*

She was a petite woman with short gray hair and a rosy face, maybe eighty years old but perky as a wily teen on a lunch date with best friends. It was a table of twelve, and she was the matriarch. She told me her name before introducing everybody else. "This is a friend, Alice, and this is her husband. And Alice's great nephew." I exchanged pleasant nods and gave Alice's red-headed toddler a little wave. But then Ann suddenly harrumphed and flapped her hand. "And I don't really know the other people." The whole table roared with laughter.

Great characters make great stories, and here was my character, my rescuer. "If you haven't had a Jones hot dog, you've never had a hot dog," Ann said, spry as a teen but with a little old lady's high thin voice—the voice was fantastic. "If you've never met at Jones with your friends, you don't have any friends." Her friends roared again.

I learned friends had been gathering at Jones for more than half a century. "We've changed nothing," said Curtis Jones, the owner back then. He was probably retirement age but still clad in a white apron and turning hot dogs on the grill. He told me his mom and dad bought the place in 1958, which at one time had been a grocery store in Clayton.

"I used to bag groceries here," quipped a man in a nearby booth, grabbing my attention—another who'd freed himself from the corner of the cushion to greet the camera.

"I guess Jones has been a part of your life your whole life?" I asked.

He held up his half-eaten dog, smothered in chili. "Just goes to show you, hot dogs are good for you."

I noticed a smiley woman with a full plate—a smile, always an encouraging sign—and asked her what she'd ordered. "A hot dog with chili, slaw, extra mustard, half an order of fries and a tea." She punched each item with a head nod. "Same every time."

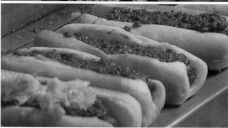

I was suddenly swimming in sound and was also struck by the atmosphere: red-checked tablecloths, iron support poles stretch-

ing from floor to ceiling around the restaurant. The poles added character, and character is what the place and my story were all about.

Character and caricatures. I spotted several figurines on the shelves, miniature hot dog men, one with his thumb up, grinning.

"Takes you back a few years," said a man at Ann's table, now holding the red-headed toddler. I figured the whippersnapper would be eating lots of hot dogs in the years to come. I had a feeling Ann already had.

"Always a big day when you come to Jones," she said in her high thin voice. "It's like coming home!"

THE GROCERY BAG

4879 NC-42, CLAYTON, NC 27527, (919) 553-4088

Six million hot dogs . . . and counting.

The Grocery Bag has actually sold well over six million now, because every day the ladies at the grill prepare hundreds more. They steam the dogs, gob them with onions and chili, wrap them, and hand them to folks in line at the counter with a, "Here ya' go. Thank ya', Hon."

Six million hot dogs. And the irony is, they're not even famous. They're almost famous.

The Grocery Bag is inside a convenience store, inside the Percy Flowers Store, and insiders claim it serves the best hot dogs in North Carolina. And though the hot dogs might not be famous, the Percy Flowers Store is.

The building is a wide, red-brick landmark at Highway 42 and Buffalo Road, six miles east of Clayton. It doesn't look anything like a convenience store, not with the dormer windows, pretty green awnings, and restored Model T permanently parked out front. People in Johnston and surrounding counties know the store. And many know the hot dog stand inside the store.

The Grocery Bag opened in 1972 and moved to its current location in '83. Tommy Fitzgerald has overseen it the whole time and remembers the man who bought the very first dog way back when. "He kinda looked at me funny and said, 'Well, are they any good?' And I said, 'These hot dogs are almost famous.'" The name stuck and the dogs sold, and today the almost-famous hot dogs are . . . well . . . famous. "We try to be known as the friendliest convenience store anywhere," Tommy says.

Even the hamburgers are big sellers. "We hand roll our burgers every day," says the burger-station lady. What an efficient assembly line behind the counter, a half-dozen diligent ladies. "Oh yeah, it flows," she says.

They ladies have fun. They kid one another and even the customers; they know most by name, and by order.

"Two all the way!" calls the order-taker lady and thanks the man in front of her. "We appreciate you," she adds with a smile, then nods to the next fellow in line. "Your usual?"

I stand to the side observing, and the observing makes me starving. I'm thinking two all the way with extra mustard when one of the hot dog makers catches my eye. "We're blessed to be here," she says, and her words ring true. I realize the grill within the store is its only little island, a happy hot dog sanctuary.

I watch her spoon onions on a chili-smothered dog, which looks amazing. But it's the word she repeats I find especially satisfying, *Blessed.*

Six million . . . and counting.

CHARLIE'S BBQ & GRILLE

**8948 CLEVELAND RD., CLAYTON, NC 27520, (919) 934-0093,
CHARLIESBBQANDGRILLE.ORG**

Charlie Carden is the Charlie of Charlie's BBQ, and he's committed to great food and excellent service—including service to the state.

He spent thirty years in law enforcement, twenty with the North Carolina Highway Patrol. He stopped many people on the road, and now they stop to see him. Charlie's barbecue is the ticket.

"We have pulled pork, beef brisket, ribs, chicken . . . " Charlie is slow talking and easy going. I bet he'd be awfully nice reading somebody their rights. He reads the menu the same way, with sincerity and respect. He tells me the barbecue is pit-cooked, seasoned on the premises, and that the sauces and rubs come from time-honored family recipes.

I read the menu myself; it's lengthy: smoked sausage, fried catfish and flounder, char-grilled burgers, hot dogs and corn dogs, chicken salad, pimento cheese sandwiches . . . And then there are the sides: collards, creamy corn, yellow squash, beer-battered onion rings, fried pickle chips . . . "We're probably putting more pounds on people in Johnston County than any other facility you can imagine," he says, grinning.

Lots of people know Charlie, and travel to rural Johnston County to eat at Charlie's BBQ & Grille. "It can get real chaotic," he says. "Sometimes I feel like I need the highway patrol to direct traffic."

Except the highway patrol is *part* of the traffic. "Oh, it's a great place to eat," says a uniformed trooper on his lunch break. In fact, the whole table is full of troopers, but the others are busy eating. "Feels like you're at home here. We're part of the family."

Pictures from Charlie's highway patrol days decorate the walls. He retired as a major in 2008 and then opened the restaurant with his wife, Kim. "I have fun every day. I'm here from 5:30 in the morning to 8:30 at night."

He shows me the kitchen and peeks at the collards, stirs the cabbage, and tells me about his barbecue sauce: Charlie's Sipping Sauce, he calls it. "They say it's so good you can drink it right out of the jar, and we put it in a Mason jar in case you want to do that." He's not serious, of course, not about people drinking it, at least I don't think so, though it is the color of iced tea.

It's good talking to Charlie—everybody talks to Charlie—and I take time to admire the highway patrol memorabilia around the restaurant, the various pictures, patches, and badges. "Reminds me of good times in my life," he says. Though I'm pretty sure the good times haven't ended for him.

The place is alive with chatter; the atmosphere is patriotic, and the food down-home: Brunswick stew, fried okra, mac & cheese, banana pudding, apple pie . . . He must work awfully hard, I think, preparing the meals and working long days.

And yet Charlie can't stop grinning. "We just have the best time here," he says—and says it with great sincerity.

REDNECK BBQ LAB

12101 NC-210 B, BENSON, NC 27504, (919) 938-8334, THEREDNECKBBQLAB.COM

What a name.

Redneck conjures up all kinds of good-ol'-boy imagery, and not necessarily flattering. And yet I must tip my hat to the fella who— Hell, yeah!—embraced his southern heritage (or rather bear-hugged it), stamped Redneck on his restaurant sign, probably thrust out his chest (and his belly, too), stuck a meaty hand to his brow, and saluted. I pictured a burly sort with a wad of tobacco in his cheek, bandana hanging half out of his back pocket, and an American flag rippling across his rumpled T-shirt. I did not expect to meet a scientist.

Redneck to me means rural, easy going, nothin' fancy but dog- gone dependable. It does not mean science, but Jerry Stephenson may be a bit of both. He opened Redneck BBQ Lab in 2017 in the McGee's Crossroads area of Johnston County, in a building that looks like a convenience store and seems to fit the restaurant's name.

"This is part of the magic that occurs," Jerry says. We're in the kitchen, watching one of his workers slice a hunk of meat. The butcher is good with the blade and surgically cuts and trims, while Jerry talks of briskets and burnt ends and the care and thought that goes into his product.

"It's this protein reaction," he says. He elaborates, but the miner- als and proteins are tough to follow—Me? I studied journalism and English—although I get the idea. There's lots of big-time techno gob- bledygook; after all, *Lab* is also part of the restaurant's name.

What is clear to me is the customers' reaction. Many tell me it's the best barbecue in North Carolina, and they talk of those burnt ends as if they've never eaten anything so good.

"Basically, it's like meat candy, super tender, sweet, and tangy," someone says, and it's an accurate description: chunky pieces coated in a glazy sauce.

"They're the cut ends off the brisket," somebody else explains. "You know, it's hard to find brisket anywhere in eastern North Carolina."

I'm receiving an education on my visit to the Redneck BBQ Lab, which I didn't expect. I hadn't expected turkey, either. Some tell me they like the turkey best of all. And then there are the ribs and Brunswick stew—but no hush puppies or french fries.

"People said you can't survive in North Carolina without french fries and hush puppies, and I said we can." Jerry also mentions his homemade bacon and tells me all about his collards. "And we're hand stripping them, actually stripping the leaves off."

But it's the barbecue he's known for—*BBQ*, the middle part of the restaurant's name that has caused the place to be slathered with accolades. I note the shiny row of tall trophies on the shelf, which includes a fat gold pig, and I think what a piggybank that would make.

I also see a rough-hewn sign on the wall and wonder if somebody copied its message out of Webster's Dictionary. And whether it will one day be added to a science manual. REDNECK: A HARDWORKING INDIVIDUAL WHO LOVES GOD, FAMILY, AND COUNTRY. AND GOOD BBQ.

Hell, yeah!

BIG STEVE'S BAGELS

12330 NC-210, BENSON, NC 27504, (919) 989-8006,
BIGSTEVESBAGELS.COM

"Two years ago, I weighed four-hundred-and-something pounds, so I was Big Steve."

Big Steve went on a diet, a big-big diet, so his family joked about changing the name of Big Steve's Bagels. "They were gonna call it Medium Steve's," Big Steve says, rolling his eyes.

Steve and his family are from Staten Island, New York, and moved to Benson in 2005. "You crazy?" cried his wife, Donna, back then. "Benson, North Carolina? You mean you couldn't find anyplace else?"

"'Fuggetaboutit,'" Steve says, mimicking his better half. "'Ya' outta ya' mind!'" A New York deli serving bagels in Benson? Johnston County? New Yorkers in the rural south? But great day in the mornin', Lawd have mercy, the deli's been draw-ing crowds from the get-go.

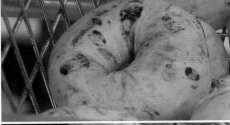

"Love it. Best bagel place around," says a man with a not-so-southern accent. "Originally from up north," he says when I ask. "You're not gonna hold that against me, are ya'?" he says and winks—I suppose his

wink is an adopted sign of southern hospitality.

Another man overhears us. "Ten out of ten," he says, though his *ten* comes out *tin. Tin out of tin.* Definitely a southerner.

"We're a family," Steve says, sweeping his arm as if addressing the litany of photographs that cover the walls, hundreds of happy customers mugging for the camera.

One of the photos shows Bob and Betsy, whose picture hangs above the salt-and-pepper shakers at their usual table; at least, I think that's them. "We were a lot younger," Bob says, and they both laugh. The two have been regulars at Big Steve's so long Bob has a bagel named after him: The Big Bad Bob. I ponder that a moment and wonder how often Bob eats the Bob while Bob looks on.

Big Steve's is an omelets-all-day kind of place. Plus bagels, of course, and subs, cannolis, and knishes. "A knish?" I ask.

"Mashed potato mixture with seasonings and spices," replies one of the cooks as she shows me a square, golden-brown patty. "Really good," she declares.

Big Steve insists everything is fresh and that the knishes, cannolis, and pork roll sandwiches are popular with everybody. "A pork roll sandwich?"

"A New Jersey thing," he says.

"Southerners love us, too," adds Donna. "Don't forget that."

Fuggetaboutit? No way, not with pictures of people in Carolina blue all around the deli. I also see plenty of New York Yankees insignias; one photo shows a bald fella with one tattooed on the back of his head. No doubt about it, Big Steve's is a melting pot. The Statue of Liberty is framed on the wall as well. *Give me your huddled masses . . .*

"Do you feel like you've found your place?" I ask Big Steve. "Benson? The store?"

"Absolutely," he says without hesitation. And though these days Big Steve looks more like Medium Steve, the grin he wears is extra large. Super-sized.

STEPHENSON'S BAR-B-Q

11964 NC-50, WILLOW SPRING, NC 27592, (919) 894-4530

Fire has eaten half the shovel.

The metal part—it's less than half the length it should be after years of scooping fiery coals. And yet it still scoops; Andy Stephenson shows me. He sticks it deep into one end of the blazing pit, hauls out a load of coals and shoves it far into the other end, beneath hunks of pig sizzling on the rack above. "I done this a many a day," he says in a country drawl that's classic Johnston County.

Andy is a big fella with a whiskery face and NC State ball cap—and a fire-eaten shovel. It was his daddy's shovel, too, and his daddy left quite an impression. Andy shows me two obvious indentations on the wooden handle. "From so many years of grabbing it by the end."

Indeed, his daddy's fingerprints are all over the restaurant. Paul Stephenson opened Stephenson's Bar-B-Q in 1958, knowing little about the business. But he did know about pigs. Paul was a Johnston County farmer. "Had good land, and he married my mama," Andy says. Paul eventually figured he could make more money cooking pigs than raising them, so he built a flat-top cinderblock building. "And they waited for that first customer, to see if they'd turn on the turn signal."

And that's when everything turned for the Stephenson family. "There was only twenty-five seats," Andy says. "And everybody laughed at Daddy, and said, 'Well, Paul, who's gonna sit in all them chairs?'"

Six decades and three additions later, Stephenson's Bar-B-Q is still blazing away. "Lookin' pretty smoky," Andy snorts, tossing another heap of coals under the pig rack—or, rather, half a heap with his half-eaten shovel.

It's hard work in the pit, a narrow dungeon well over a hundred degrees. Andy drags a dirty hand across his forehead, knocking back the brim of his cap. "I don't believe I need an iPhone to cook a pig."

It's a great snippet of sound and seems to say something about the place. "We're about hard work and good faith," Andy says. "If it ain't broke, we just don't fix it."

I meet all kinds of friendly people inside the restaurant—and catch a much-needed breather from the smoky pit. People exclaim over the barbecue and barbecue chicken. "It just falls off the bone," says the kitchen girl, scooping syrupy pieces of chicken onto a plate. Turns out, she's Andy's daughter, a pretty brunette with dimples on her cheeks that wink when she smiles. "There's just a lot of history," she says. "That's what I love about it."

It's what her dad loves, too. Andy shows me one of the restaurant's original signs, an old wooden board with cracked red paint that reads, CLOSED SUNDAY. "That's because Granny always said no money you took in on Sunday would do you no good."

He flips through a stack of snapshots, many of his daddy, and talks fondly of his mama and everything his folks built. "We're truly

blessed," he says in a tone quite different from before, full of sentiment and love. Stephenson's has endured. The fire still burns.

Back in the pit room, Andy shovels more coal but doesn't seem to mind the heat and smoke. Or the half-eaten shovel. A regular shovel rests in the corner, unused. After a moment, he takes a break, leans on the half-shovel's wooden handle, and wraps his fingers over his daddy's indentations. "When you cook pig all day," he says, "your dog likes you when you get home."

CRICKET'S GRILL

506 E. MARKET ST., SMITHFIELD, NC 27577, (919) 934-0938

It wasn't what I expected.

I had heard so much about the hot dog place in Smithfield. People kept emailing me, telling me Cricket's Grill had the best, best hot dogs in the state. Smithfield is just a half-hour drive from Raleigh, and I figured I'd do a story someday. But the somedays kept drifting by.

I was embarrassed when I finally called—though, better late than never. The fractured voice on the other end seemed rushed, breathless, but said come anytime. At least I thought that's what she said. She had a hard time pronouncing Tar Heel Traveler, and when she repeated it back with a question mark, I felt oddly comforted: *Tar Heel Traveler?* I had no need to be embarrassed after all; the place hadn't missed me a bit.

All those emails oozing with warmth and nostalgia had me picturing a white picket fence, striped awning over a front door, and an American flag hung from a porch beam. But what I found was just a trailer, that's it, like a trailer-park trailer, only bright yellow, and the lady passing food out the window was certainly not a Johnston County native. She was Asian, and so was most of the staff inside the trailer, cooking burgers and dogs and wrapping them, lickety split, in wax paper. Not a southern drawl to be heard in the group.

"I raised in Thailand," said the woman in charge. "That's why I cannot speak too good English."

Blair was her name, or her Americanized name, and she had a radiant smile and could wrap a dog in half a second. "No education, no job, no money," she said when I asked why she left her native land. She had moved to America years earlier after marrying a man from North Carolina and couldn't speak English when she arrived. "Even my husband, we sign language," she said, laughing.

Back then, Blair had found a job at Cricket's Grill. "I didn't know the dime, the nickel, what they looked like." But she learned quickly and gained confidence. And then, just weeks after she was hired, the grill's owner decided to sell, figured Blair could make a go of it, and together they struck a sensible deal.

It was risky; Blair took a chance—but one that had obviously paid off in the years since. I marveled at the never-ending line at the window. And I soon realized those weren't just burgers and dogs passing from one set of hands to the next but something else entirely. Something totally unexpected: egg rolls.

"Egg rolls?" I asked. "In Johnston County?"

"Ancient secret recipe," Blair said and gave me one to try. She also gave me her radiant smile, and if there ever was a smile that said, "American Dream," it was hers. She glowed—and so did the egg roll, crispy golden brown. I took a healthy bite, and it was fantastic.

Not what I expected at all.

DOUG SAULS
BBQ AND SEAFOOD

813 WESTERN AVE., NASHVILLE, NC 27856, (252) 459-2310

It's tough to say which is more popular, the meat or the fish.

"Sometimes I tell people I don't know if we're a barbecue or seafood restaurant because we do a lot of both," Steve Sauls tells me with a shake of his bald head.

Steve's dad opened the restaurant in 1977 in Nashville, North Carolina. A man named Shorty hired on soon after. Shorty is short but fast. He takes orders at the walk-up counter, scribbles on a pad, punches the register, changes money, and has his pencil poised for the next person in line. "So you've worked here over forty years?" I ask.

"I've worked here so long I stopped counting," he mumbles and starts scribbling again—his pencil is little more than a nub.

The place is rustic and creaky in a comforting way. "The authentic barbecue joint," says a man in a cowboy hat. But then somebody else tells me they come here for the shrimp. And actually, the chicken might rival them both. Steve says he goes through twenty-five cases of chicken a week, and when he shakes his bald head again, I figure that must be a load, especially since the restaurant is open just Thursday through Saturday; Sunday through Wednesday is family time. Then again, Steve's whole family works at Sauls, so family time is seven days straight.

"Ticket number fifty-six!"

Orders are coming and going quick; in fact, the take-out area might be busier than the sit-down section. A man at a table sums it up nicely. He wears a blue work shirt, a mechanic or truck driver maybe, and sits by himself at a corner table. "It's some of that grandma's old-fashioned cookin'," he says with a crispy half-eaten chicken leg between his fingers. "And my three sides of vegetables, have to have that." I spot a stray green bean under his fork, but otherwise the veggies have already vanished. "And that good old-fashioned sweet tea."

The man may be alone in a corner, but he sure looks like he's in heaven. His face is as shiny as his plate, which he's scraped clean except for the chicken crumbs. "Ain't too many places like this right here." He takes another bite and chews. "When you find a spot like this, it's well worth it."

He finishes the chicken leg, sighs, and sits back in his chair, and I figure he's either completely content or longs for another leg. Either way his face is *brighter* than his plate; by now he's collected the crumbs and eaten them, too. "Grandma's old-fashioned cookin'," he says.

BROAD STREET DELI & MARKET

129 E. BROAD ST., DUNN, NC 28334, (910) 891-1002, BROADSTREETDELIANDMARKET.COM

Jamie is so sweet and nice. I think that's largely why her gourmet deli is so successful. Gourmet? Successful? In Dunn?

It's a quiet town in Harnett County with a population fewer than ten thousand. "Were you worried at first?" I ask her.

Jamie's blue eyes pop. "Absolutely!"

Jamie Adkins grew up working in restaurants, ten years waiting tables, and met her husband, Jeff, a self-taught cook. In 2005, they bought an old building in downtown Dunn, a place that had been a drugstore a hundred years earlier. "We just jumped in with a lot of faith and both feet."

And two little hands. Even Jamie's son helped renovate the building back then. She shows me snapshots of young Riley cradling a paintbrush. "When I think about my little five-year-old when we opened who's in college now it makes me very proud."

Today, Riley even has a sandwich named for him. "The Life of Riley is roast beef, melted brie cheese, and homemade plum sauce on a toasted croissant," Jamie says, and I can tell by the light in her eyes that she's proud of both her son and his sandwich.

I feel proud of Jamie myself, the chance she took and her years of success. She's the face of Broad Street Deli & Market, the smiling face; husband Jeff is more behind the scenes.

I admire the deli's artful decorations and tasteful display of North Carolina products—I remind myself to buy some Aunt Ruby's Peanuts before I leave. Sunlight streams through the front windows, and there's a cozy elegance about the place, everything clean and well cared for.

Jamie asks me what I'd like to eat: Turkey Reuben, Chicken Salad, Pimento Cheese sandwich . . . So many choices. "Anything you want," she says.

"Anything you want," echoes a man seated nearby who offers to buy me lunch. I recognize the ruddy face beneath the brim of his hat, a fella I interviewed some time ago on another story nearby; I even remember his name.

"Cecil."

"Salad," he says. "I love her salads." He shows me a shelf with bottles of Jamie's Poppyseed Dressing and tells me how scrumptious it is, just the right sweetness, and says he's sure I'll see it in stores across the US one day. "She's remarkable."

"But does it surprise you?" I ask, "That a gourmet deli can survive in Dunn?"

He shrugs. "Not really," he says and invites me to look around. The restaurant is full, even though it's past the normal lunch hour, and everyone seems pleasantly relaxed.

"It's the team I've got behind me," Jamie says. "And I meet so many nice people." Her smile spreads. And so has the deli's popularity, thanks in part to *Southern Living*, which once highlighted the restaurant in its magazine. Today, curious travelers routinely pull off Interstate 95 to investigate. And to eat.

"Don't forget the carrot cake," Cecil says. "I love her carrot cake."

Jamie continually checks on tables. "Everything good?" She thanks people and smiles, always smiles. The deli is thriving. Gourmet in Dunn.

"It's just a good feeling," she says. "A great community and great group of people."

SHERRY'S BAKERY

**122 N. WILSON AVE., DUNN, NC 28334, (910) 892-3310,
SHERRYSBAKERY.WIXSITE.COM/SHERRYSBAKERY**

It's the sweetest smelling corner in town.

"Good, good, good, good!" Freddie Williford talks as if he's had too much sugar, and maybe he has, but I think his enthusiasm has more to do with how much he loves his job and how proud he is of the good, good, good-ies spread in front of him. "Honey buns, chocolate honey buns, chocolate nut honey buns . . . "

We're in the back of Sherry's Bakery, a huge space with ovens, coolers, and trays full of cream-filled oatmeal cookies and chocolate covered doughnuts. The sweetest smelling corner in Dunn has a sweet spot, and we're in the thick of it.

"What we call a long john and a chocolate biscuit," Freddie says, pointing to two other trays loaded with plump pastries.

"People come here from all over everywhere," Freddie says. He's in his eighties, bald but for white wisps on the sides of his head, and yet his enthusiasm is—fresh. "Look, freshness is the key to success in a bakery," he says. "Fresh, fresh, fresh, fresh!"

Freddie and his wife, Mary, bought the bakery in 1967 and named it after their oldest daughter. But Sherry's is more than just a bakery.

"Ham biscuits, sausage biscuits."

"Bacon and egg sandwich."

"Delicious chicken salad."

I've moseyed up to a table of men who list their mealtime favorites. The bakery is also a restaurant, a sizeable one. "We call this the Wisdom Club," one of the men says. "But it only takes one vote to get in, and you can vote for yourself." The whole group breaks out laughing.

I interview a woman in a booth who looks close to Freddie's age. "I've come here all my life," she says. "In fact, my wedding cake came from here."

Wedding cakes, birthday cakes, holiday pies . . . Sherry's has provided so many delicious memories over the years, and the woman in the booth echoes that. She tells me people feel a sentimental attachment to the bakery and that the feelings run deep. "The sweetest smelling corner in town," she says, which is an obvious way to end my story on Sherry's.

But instead I give Freddie the final word, and he enthusiastically captures the essence of the bakery, its meaning, the sweetness at its center. And curiously, it has less to do with the good, good, goodies that are fresh, fresh, fresh.

"Fine people," Freddie says. "That's what I love about it. The people."

GRANNY'S DONUTS

201 JOHNSON ST., ABERDEEN, NC 28315, (910) 944-9401

A quirky clock hangs on the wall at Granny's.

It's a flat wooden board with skinny hands, glittery numbers, and a sign that reads, FRESH DONUTS AT 5. AND IT'S ALWAYS 5! Every glittery number is 5.

Fresh donuts all the time—or maybe not. Another sign reads, WE CLOSE EARLY IF WE SELL OUT.

I work the mic around a table of early risers. This is Moore County, land of retirees, many from the North and Midwest who've migrated south to settle near the golf courses around Pinehurst, or here in Aberdeen where they've found the perfect place to start their day. "Our regular meeting," says a man in the middle.

"The place to be in the morning," says the woman across from him.

It's a table of ten, and nobody seems in a hurry to go anywhere. "There's plenty of work to do at home," the woman says, "but more fun coming here."

They're from different parts of the country, I can hear it in their accents—New York, Boston, Wisconsin—but they all agree the donuts are fabulous. "Wicked good," says the Bostonian. "Especially the coconut ones," pipes the Minnesotan. The Manhattan man in the middle raves about the jelly donuts. A cinnamon bun is another fella's favorite.

The owners, meanwhile, are up at the front, a husband and wife working the counter and drive-through. The wife's name is B.

"B, like the letter?" I ask. "They just call you B?"

"B, yes. Sometimes Bumblebee."

She's a busy bee, a petite woman constantly boxing up donuts but always with a smile. Even some of the donuts wear smiles, glazy grins. B is the donut decorator, apparently with a sweet sense of humor, and she also migrated to Aberdeen from distant parts, as did her husband, Vina.

"I took over for my parents," Vina says in a sing-song dialect. His parents were from Laos and found their way to America, and eventually to North Carolina, and ran the donut shop for more than twenty years. Vina and B tell me how happy they are to be operating Granny's now, though they admit it's hard work. *Fresh donuts at 5. And it's always 5!*

The morning is drifting by, but customers continue to come and go. Well, except for the table of early risers who are also late stayers.

"There's something special about Granny's that surpasses the donut," says the woman from Wisconsin, and her friends around the table nod in agreement. They're from many corners of the country, brought together by the little donut shop run by the sweet couple with Asian origins.

"It's like when you go home to a family reunion," the Wisconsin woman says, and I detect emotion in her accent. "You get that every day here." She looks around at the others, still nodding. "I just love Granny's."

It's clear she speaks for everyone.

PIK-N-PIG

194 GILLIAM MCCONNELL RD., CARTHAGE, NC 28327,
(910) 947-7591, PIK-N-PIG.COM

All these restaurant stories . . .

People say they envy me: traveling, eating, getting paid for it. But every story is a challenge, nothing is ever simple. While nibbling on my doughnut or biscuit, hot dog or hamburger, barbecue or steak, I'm thinking about what else I need, what other interviews, what video, what words—I hope I find the right words.

It's easy for one restaurant story to blur with another, to resemble another—and another—especially in the way they're written and edited; fast pace, quick edits, and punchy writing is the norm. But the last thing I want is for them to look and sound the same, so I dig for what's different and distinct. I eat and think and worry.

What a relief, then, to visit the Pik-n-Pig in Carthage. No worries at all because the story is right in front of me. Right above me.

The sky is full of planes, one- and two-seater single props, buzzing around and landing at the restaurant. It's a restaurant with an airstrip—or is it an airstrip with a restaurant?

"Well, the airstrip came first," Roland Gilliam tells me. He's the owner, a burly fella with a gray mustache whose denim shirt and hat are embroidered with airplane emblems. "I always wanted my own airport, so I started building me an airport." He paved the runway in 1994, and the place took off.

"Oh, look, look."

"Oh, my gosh!"

I mic two ladies seated in lawn chairs, thrilled by the planes buzzing by them. "Oh, here he comes, here he comes!" A plane touches down only feet away.

"Whoo!"

"Oh, that's got to be a ten on the scale."

"Magnificent!"

The women look to be in their seventies and are so excited they kick their feet with each landing like little kids and don't score anybody less than eight. I'm so taken by the planes myself I almost forget about the barbecue.

"Live coals. No gas, no electricity," says the skinny chef. He's cooking outside on a steamy grill with a revolving rack full of huge chunks of pork, so dark they're almost black; I can practically taste the crispy skin. But the best part, he assures me, is the 'cue itself: moist, tender and packed with flavor. I wonder why the chef is so skinny, although I'm sure he must be so occupied by the barbecue and mesmerized by the airplanes that he probably forgets to eat.

I wander inside to place my order. It's a big place with a row of windows facing the airstrip. It's crowded, and all eyes seem to be fixed outside, including mine, and so I decide to wait on lunch—and on a window seat.

I exit the building and see a pilot hopping from his Cessna. He grabs his helmet and heads for the restaurant, and we meet halfway. "It's more fun than you can image," he tells me. "I have a

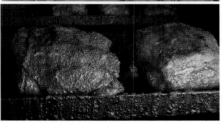

passion for flying and a passion for barbecue, and that's why this is a good mix."

"Look, look!"

"Oh, my!"

The two lawn-chair ladies remain enthralled—and curious. "I wonder what the food does to their tummies," one muses as we watch a pilot climb back in his plane carrying a doggy bag. "Maybe the gas quotient changes." They both howl with laughter and kick their feet.

The aircraft taxis, gains speed and lifts off without a wobble: smooth, beautiful, magnificent. "It just doesn't get any better than this," one of the ladies says. None of us can peel our eyes from the plane; we watch it grow smaller and smaller in the cloudless sky.

A ten indeed.

YARBOROUGH'S ICE CREAM

**132 MCIVER ST., SANFORD, NC 27330, (919) 776-6266,
YARBOROUGHS-HOMEMADE-ICE-CRM.BUSINESS.SITE**

The ice cream is homemade and has been since 1935.

The man who founded Yarborough's Ice Cream, Phil Yarborough, started as a dairy farmer in Lee County. "He was the first one in this area to have pasteurized milk," says his son, Carol, who's pushing eighty and laughs at his girlie name, chuckling about how times have changed. "Who names their son Carol nowadays?"

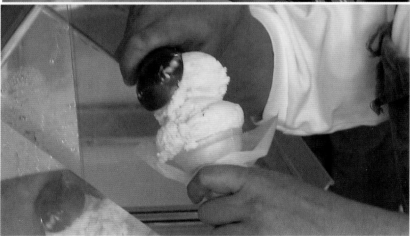

He's right; times change, and his dad changed with them. Phil began using milk from his dairy to make ice cream for the public, and in time Yarborough's Ice Cream in Sanford became—"The greatest place in Lee County," says a man with a double scoop of Katie's Chocolate Malt. Or is it Mollie's Follies? A few flavors are named after Yarborough grandchildren; the shop has remained in the family. Carol ran it for years after his dad died, and now his two sons scoop and cook. Burgers and fries are on the menu, too.

"Not much has changed at all," Tim Yarborough tells me, and, well, maybe times *don't* change. He says the shop is pretty much like it's always been: the grill, ice cream counter, a few tables and booths, the place bright and simple. Tim is Carol's son, a tall redhead. "Cookies and cream is good," he says. "Bubblegum's good. Strawberry cheesecake is popular." Apparently, the flavors *have* changed. I can't imagine Granddad Phil making cheesecake and bubblegum ice cream. "They're all good," Tim insists.

"I give it my best," says his brother, Michael, who's in the back making the ice cream, mixing and weighing it. He's a rail of a fella who, despite his thin frame, is careful to sample it often so he gets it just right. "I want to please the customer. I try to carry on the family tradition."

The building itself celebrates that tradition. A colorful mural of Phil's old Fairview Dairy is painted on the side, believed to be the first 3-D mural in North Carolina. One of the black-and-white cows appears to poke his nose at passersby. Or maybe he's just sniffing the ice cream.

I could use some myself, a scoop or two—or three. Wonder what Mollie's Follie tastes like. Or Katie's Chocolate Malt.

JOHNSON'S DRIVE-IN

1520 E. 11TH ST., SILER CITY, NC 27344

The proof is not just in the food. Sometimes it's also in the dumpster.

Claxton Johnson leads me to the back of the building, stands on his tiptoes, and drags a flattened cardboard box out of the big brown garbage bin. He flips the box over, finds the flap with the bar code, and jabs his finger at the bold stamp on the stickered label. "USDA," he says. "Best meat you can buy." Okay, I get the point, but to be honest I'd rather sample it with my mouth than smell it by the dumpster. He thankfully leads me inside.

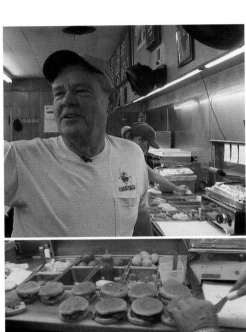

There's a row of booths by the windows with a view of the street, and opposite them a counter stretches from one wall to the other. Claxton takes his place at the grill, snags a spatula and begins mashing the burgers, which sizzle and spit. And now the best part: He tops them with a thick square hunk of Velveeta cheese, and talk about smell—this is more like it. "Delicious, delicious," he says, and I'm impressed by his giddy enthusiasm after all these years.

His folks opened Johnson's in 1946. "And I been here the whole time," he says. "I was a little boy out there catching curb." He means back when Johnson's was a drive-in and he took burgers out to the cars. The curb service eventually went away, but the customers never did.

"Haven't you heard?" asks Claxton's daughter, Carolyn, a spunky redhead who works behind the counter, too. "The best cheeseburgers you'll ever get."

From the looks of them, I think she might be right. Oh my gosh, those thick yellow-orange hunks of Velveeta melting and dripping down the sides . . . my mouth waters. "You're gonna have to try one in a minute," Claxton says. "Then you'll know for yourself."

What I do know as I watch Claxton mash the sizzling burgers, is that time hasn't yet squashed the place. Johnson's has hung on: same family, same food, and many of the same customers. "He gets the best meat," a man at the counter tells me. "The best." I hope the fella doesn't feel the need to prove it by showing me to the dumpster.

Carolyn slides me my lunch and leans on the counter, eager to witness my first bite, and even Claxton turns to look, spatula suspended in air. I pick up the burger with both hands, and it's just the way I like it, dripping with juice and cheesy—very, very cheesy. Here goes.

I sink in my teeth. And savor the applause.

CAROLINA RESTAURANT

260 STOCKYARD RD., SILER CITY, NC 27344, (919) 663-6032

It's a restaurant and cattle auction. Beef in the ring and on the griddle, all under one roof.

The place hollers CAROLINA STOCKYARDS in giant letters across the top of the wide brick building in Siler City. I walk through the double glass doors into the lobby and am torn over whether to turn right or left; there are other doors at each end.

An odd mix of odors mingles in the middle. Up through my nose flows sizzling meat, hay, and manure. The manure doesn't bother me; it reminds me of cowboys, and I wish I'd worn my knockoff Stetson and fake snakeskin boots.

I at last hook my thumbs to my belt loops and pivot toward the manure smell and a sing-song chant echoing on the right-hand side. I kick open the door with my sneaker and walk bowlegged into an open ring.

The seating is auditorium style with an elevated stage up front where an auctioneer is rattling away behind a microphone. Numbers roll off his tongue, and I'm in awe; me, a fella used to a mic, but this buckaroo is a master, no hesitation or skipping a beat. Rat-a-tat-tat. And yet, the cowpokes in front of him sit rather nonchalantly, boots propped against seat backs in front of them. One of the nonchalants lifts a lazy finger, and the sing-song stops cold. "Sold!" The big board flashes $2,106. The lazy man just bought himself a heifer, a small black one, which trots obliviously around a caged ring.

Two grand and change? I think. *Who are these guys?* A wrinkly-faced fella in the crowd tells me they're buyers hired by huge farms out west. "Big money," he whispers, while the auction rattles on. I thank him but resist shaking his hand. No false moves. I don't think my spaniels back home would take kindly to a cow.

I believe I could stand here for hours watching and listening, but it's the burgers and steaks I've come for—best not to think where they come *from*—and so I saunter back to the lobby and push through the door on the opposite side.

The Carolina Restaurant has its own kind of rhythm, a steady murmur that's a mix of happy chit-chat and scraping spatulas. The place isn't big on atmosphere, and yet that's what makes the atmosphere: spartan, like a restaurant in a stockyard should be. I breathe in and am suddenly famished—and forgetful—the cuts on the grill overwhelm the memories of the bulls in the ring. I wanna eat.

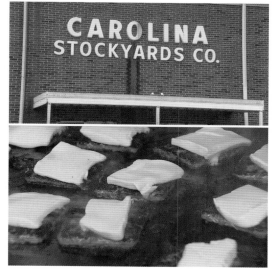

"Do people come for the cattle auction or the food?" I ask a man lounging in a seat. Both, he says and tells me he's here every Monday and Friday, auction days. He watches over there, wanders over here.

There's plenty of denim in the restaurant: ranchers, cowboys, cowhands. One fella wears a cap with swirly black-and-white splotches, and I'm sure the Chick-fil-A cows would hate this place. "Is it strange having a restaurant next to a stockyard?" I ask him.

"Not really. You know, farmers gotta eat, too."

I notice a few families, including one with a curly-haired woman and gaggle of kids. The table is a crisscross of little arms reaching for french fries, ketchup, and Cokes—and, I hope, napkins. "Friday is the day to go to the stockyard," the lady says, "and have a hamburger and make sure you keep your hands down while you're at the auction. Don't wiggle, don't touch your ears or anything." She giggles, no doubt grateful an unintended bull hasn't added to her confusion.

What an unusual place, I think: live cows, grilled steaks, and an aura of excitement at both ends of the building.

After a while, I walk outside, bowlegged. The parking lot is packed with pickups and trailers, and beside the building is a cow pen, and I decide to climb the catwalk. Good looking bulls down there, hefty ones, too, jostling around, probably sold already and on their way to Wyoming or Montana or somewhere with endless fields and a big sky. Strange to say, especially after the burger I've devoured, but I envy them and the journey that awaits.

I'd like to head west a spell myself. I'd ride into the sunset—with my knockoff Stetson and fake snakeskin boots.

MERRITT'S GRILL

**1009 S. COLUMBIA ST., CHAPEL HILL, NC 27514, (919) 942-4897,
MERRITTSBLT.COM**

Piles of bacon. No scrimpin' on the bacon.

Double bacon. Triple bacon. "More bacon!" shouts the manager.
"Whoo hoo!" He claps his hands, throws back his head, laughs, and
the laughter ripples right down the line, to all the people in line. They
laugh and cackle. And crackle and pop. This place is sizzling. "Whoo!"

Merritt's is the place to be for a BLT. The sign outside means what
it says: WORLD FAMOUS BLT'S, and it seems half the world is clogging the
parking lot. The other sign indicates traffic jam for the long haul: BLT'S
UNDER CONSTRUCTION ALL DAY LONG!

And yet the building at the corner is used to the stop-and-go.
Merritt's opened as a gas station in 1929 and later became a convenience store. Then along came Robin Britt who bought the place in

1991, together with her husband. "I would just make these huge BLTs for him." And he, in turn, began making huge BLTs at the store. "Love is a many splendored thing, isn't it?"

Well, it's a many *layered* thing at Merritt's. "Triple on rye, please!" belts the manager. "Another triple on wheat, please!" The orders pile in, and the bacon piles on. The sandwiches are mountains, the kitchen a mole hill. Half a dozen ladies scurry around that tiny space, cooking, piling, cutting, wrapping. BLTs under construction—"Double on white, please!"—all day long.

"Best kept secret of Chapel Hill," a man in line tells me, his hand half over his mouth. But clearly, the secret is out; the line stretches all the way to the door.

Another man, who evidently heard the first man secretly telling me the secret, leans toward me and says, "You stand in line, you meet people from everywhere."

Man 3 overhears and tells me he's from California, visiting his daughter who's a student at UNC. "And I had to stop at Merritt's." No doubt, he'll order a triple—California's a long way for a single.

I squeeze my way to the front, eager to interview the colorful manager. "Triple on white, please!" I want to know how much bacon he goes through in a day, but as I wait for a break between shouts, Man 4 in line starts telling me about tomatoes. "Gotta have a good tomato, and this guy does not play around with the tomatoes."

"Sixty pounds of bacon a day," the manager says, and even claps, when I finally toss him the question. I gather sixty pounds must be a heap, but I ask the follow-up anyway.

"Sixty pounds, is that a lot?"

"Sounds like a lot to me," he says and throws back his head and laughs. And then shouts. "Double on wheat, please!"

Raleigh is not far from Chapel Hill, but I order a triple anyway—I want the full experience. The manager laughs and claps and belts out the order to the ladies.

And follows it with, "Whoo hoo!"

MAMA DIP'S KITCHEN

408 W. ROSEMARY ST., CHAPEL HILL, NC 27516, (919) 942-5837, MAMADIPS.COM

Mama Dip died in May 2018. I remember her well.

Mildred "Mama Dip" Council was eighty-five years old when I met her at Mama Dip's Kitchen in 2014. She sat scrunched in the corner of the kitchen, cutting broccoli stems. The corner didn't seem big enough for such a tall lanky woman. The broccoli was bunched in a pan resting on her lap, and she kept trying to stretch her long legs, which threatened to upset the balance—and the broccoli heads. "That's why they call me Mama Dip," she said. She explained it was because of her height, because growing up on a farm she was tall enough to reach into the rain barrel and dip out water. "Ha, ha!" She hooted when she told me the story, and, wow, that smile of hers— it was plenty long, too, and had absolutely no trouble stretching; it spread from ear to ear.

Mama Dip grew up in Chatham County and started cooking as a kid. "My papa learned us how to cook," she said. And also how to pick. "He'd tell me to go pick something to eat—and he didn't say cook a steak!" She burst out laughing again.

She was resourceful in her youth and learned to eek out a living. She cooked for fraternity and sorority houses in Chapel Hill and then one day in 1976 opened her own little place, starting with just a few eggs, that was it. "Somebody opened the door and said, 'Is you open?' And I said, 'Yeah, come on in.' And I had customers all day."

And customers every day from then on. "You've become famous," I said.

"I don't call it famous." She stopped cutting the broccoli a moment. "Well, I don't know what to call it. Ha, ha!"

People often call it *The Best Southern Food*. I noticed that very slogan hanging in the restaurant lobby the day I was there. I also saw pictures of Mama Dip with well-known politicians—she usually towered over them. There was even a picture of her and President George W. Bush.

Also in the lobby were shelves full of Mama Dip's Barbecue Sauce, her special corn bread mix, and poppy seed dressing. She'd also written two cookbooks.

"Frying chicken was my thing," she said, and I gathered she was known for fried chicken. "We have greens every day, turnip greens or collard greens, black-eyed peas, and I make a cobbler. I make things that old people like. Ha!"

I loved seeing that enormous smile of hers; it was made for a TV camera, and her smile is how I remember Mama Dip. Mama Dip's Kitchen remembers her, too, for the restaurant still operates after her death, and her pictures still hang on the walls. HOMETOWN HERO reads one of the framed newspaper clippings. A hero she was. And still is.

Her legacy stretches a long, long way.

AL'S BURGER SHACK

516 W. FRANKLIN ST., CHAPEL HILL, NC 27516, (919) 904-7659, ALSBURGERSHACK.COM

The best burger in America.

In 2018, TripAdvisor bestowed that honor on the Bobo Chili Cheeseburger at Al's Burger Shack in Chapel Hill. The burger comes topped with chili sauce, coleslaw, onions, mustard, and American cheese. "Oh, it's good," Al admits. "Crazy, right?" He can barely believe it: the best in the US, the Bobo. It's listed on the shack's menu, up on the burger board, along with the Mookie, the Paco, the Kenny J., the Melly Mel, and others. "Oh, we have a lot of wacky burgers," Al says. Some come with jalapenos and bacon-onion jam. Wacky and wild but apparently wonderful.

"Just something about the quality of the ingredients that are cleaner and lighter," says a woman at a patio table. The covered patio offers a view of Franklin Street, of people strolling by or pedaling past, often decked in baby blue, UNC insignias stamped on their T-shirts. It's a college-town atmosphere, and the fun seeps into the atmosphere at Al's.

"You know, funky little place like this," Al says and once again seems like he can barely believe it, the burger shack's popularity. "Very fortunate."

Al is Al Bowers. He grew up in Greensboro and enrolled at UNC in the mid-eighties, then stayed in Chapel Hill after college and became a restaurant manager. He'd always enjoyed cooking—and eating burgers and fries. "That's always been my favorite meal." When space opened on West Franklin Street, he took a chance—so did his wife, Melody, who supported and encouraged him. They opened Al's Burger Shack on September 18, 2013, National Cheeseburger Day.

"From day one, we had a line out the door," Melody says. I ask her what the secret has been, figuring she'd say the burgers: the Bobo, the Kenny J, Sean's Bacon Cheeseburger—I want to know who Bobo, Kenny J., and Sean are. But instead she says Al; *he's* the secret. "Al. He's never met a stranger."

"Come on in, we got you, we got you." Al greets folks at the door. "Good, good." He talks to people at their tables. "Mariaaaa!" He sings to a lady at the counter. "I just met a girl named Mariaaaa!" Maria giggles and places her order—and I wonder if a Maria Burger might make it on the menu one day: The Singing Maria.

"It's just a friendly, friendly place," a man with a Classic tells me: lettuce, tomato, red onion, pickle, American cheese, and Al's special sauce.

Another fella shows me his burger, which is draped with a fried egg and piled with—Fritos. "Fritos?"

He nods and tells me it's called the San Felipe, and I wonder who San Felipe is—or where it is. "Can't wait to bite it," he says. "I'm stoked."

"Everybody's happy," says the lady sitting with him, and I have to agree. There's an enthusiastic energy about the place. And there's Al, laughing, shaking hands, patting backs. And praising his staff, his cooks, some who've been with him since the beginning—and who don't have much room to work. It is a shack, after all, and the team must grill all those burgers in tight quarters, plus juggle a bevy of ingredients.

"Cheerwine on a burger?"

The boy I ask at a table

tells me he orders it every time; Cheerwine BBQ sauce is one of Al's wild and wacky ingredients. The boy is barely a teenager, but his T-shirt is baby blue, too, and I have a feeling UNC is in his future—as are many more trips to Al's. He grips his burger with both hands and chows. Happy. The kid is definitely happy.

And so is Al, happy and humble. "Very fortunate," he says again. "Very fortunate, absolutely."

YE OLDE WAFFLE SHOPPE

173 E. FRANKLIN ST., CHAPEL HILL, NC 27514, (919) 929-9192, YEOLDEWAFFLESHOPPE.COM

I visited in 2012. But when I walked in, it was 1972.

What a crazy day at Ye Olde Waffle Shoppe in Chapel Hill, its fortieth anniversary, and the restaurant was whooping it up with a throwback to yesterday, selling everything on the board at forty-year-old prices, one day only. No surprise, the place was packed to the rafters.

Ye Olde is well known for breakfast, and there I was, waiting for a seat, squeezed against the wall but with a clear shot of the grill, drooling over omelets and biscuits, waffles and pancakes. And not just plain old pancakes but with what seemed like a basket of blueberries smooshed in the dough.

A kid sitting at the counter in front of me was just starting in on an M&M waffle with so many M&Ms, his plate looked like Christmas. A pretty brunette sat beside him, their elbows touching. UNC students obviously, boyfriend and girlfriend probably. I tapped his shoulder and asked how much the waffle cost; it filled the entire

dish. He said fifty cents and that hers cost the same. The girl's brown eyes bulged at her chocolate-chip pancake, and I doubted she'd finish half.

The two ate and giggled and never once checked their cell phones. I tell you, it *felt* like 1972. And yet I found myself pondering the future, wishing the best for this young couple once they stepped outside into the present.

I shot a glance at the door; the line looked two blocks long, and I wondered how many kids had cut class. But there was one person who wasn't there—and yet he was everywhere. Jimmy's face graced the back of the staff's T-shirts: a caricature of Jimmy Chris with his trademark eyeglasses, holding a spatula.

I met Jimmy's wife, Linda, also wearing a Jimmy T-shirt, and she filled me in on the restaurant's history. Jimmy had built the building using wood from the church they were married in back in 1968. "So when you look at the timber and brick, it's from the Greek Orthodox Church in Winston-Salem," she said, and I took a moment to admire the exposed brick and cross-timbered beams above the booths. "So, literally, Jimmy built his history into the building."

She explained how proud he was of the restaurant. "It has been incredible," she said. "And it is a very bittersweet anniversary because Jimmy planned today." Jimmy had died unexpectedly eight months earlier at age seventy-one.

"I miss him a lot," said one of the longtime staff ladies, balancing full plates in each hand. She was about to deliver them but stopped to offer a kind word. "He was my best friend."

Jimmy's daughter, Daisy, had become Ye Olde's general manager and told me how much her dad would have loved this day, the crazy busyness of it. "I'm proud of my parents," she said. "Forty years is pretty amazing on Franklin Street, and we want to continue it for years to come."

But actually, I didn't want to think of the years to come, or even of the afternoon ahead. I simply wanted to savor the moment.

I snagged a seat at last, and my bacon and eggs came cooked to perfection. I'd be sure to leave a nice tip—which would probably amount to more than the bill.

1972. Happy times indeed. Simpler ones, too.

ZACK'S HOT DOGS

201 W. DAVIS ST., BURLINGTON, NC 27215, (336) 226-4746,
ZACKSHOTDOGS.COM

His arm is a human shelf.

A half-dozen hot dogs are lined from wrist to elbow like squishy paperbacks between bookends. The server's other arm is the workhorse. His free hand grips a spoon, dips it in chili, and slathers the dogs. Then comes slaw, onions, mustard, the works piled on down the line. The man is fast, and the dogs are ready. He loads them on a tray, stretches his arm again, and the human shelf is set for another round. Another row.

Zack's Hot Dogs is named for Zack Touloupas who found his way to North Carolina from Greece and in 1928 bought a place in Burlington called Alamance Hot Weiner Lunch. It consisted of eight bar stools and four tables—the tables were actually old school desks. The restaurant sat across from City Hall, and a local fella named Scott would stop by every chance he could, especially after deciding to run for governor. He believed the hot dogs gave him luck, and maybe they did. Governor Kerr Scott won the vote.

"Do you remember the old place?"

"Oh, yeah. We used to live above it."

I'm sitting in a booth with Zack's son, John, who's in his nineties now and remembers the old place well. Maybe too well. He tells me his hours were five in the morning till two in the morning.

He started working at the restaurant in 1946, took over years later when his dad retired, and in 1977 built a new Zack's around the corner, which is where I am now. And where a second Zack is, too: John's son, another Zack Touloupas.

The younger Zack looks about my age and today runs the restaurant with his wife. "I started working here when I was five years old," he says and tells me about his grandfather's secret hot sauce and chili. "For eighty-some years we've had the same recipe."

But not the same seating. The eight bar stools and four school desks are long gone. The place is much bigger than the original, and good thing. It's packed and the crowd chatty.

"Best hot dogs."

"As good as you gonna get."

"Real nice people."

"One learned from his daddy, and the other learned from *his* daddy."

Zack, Sr.'s picture hangs on the wall. John enjoys his lunch in the booth. And the younger Zack greets everybody who walks in.

The server, meanwhile, arms himself with a fresh row, never uttering a word. Talking might jiggle the human shelf.

SOUTHERN SMOKE BBQ

29 WARREN ST., GARLAND, NC 28441, (910) 549-7484,
SOUTHERNSMOKEBBQNC.COM

It's open just two days a week: Thursday and Friday.

Best to reserve ribs Tuesday or Wednesday. "We were out of ribs today in twenty minutes," says the owner's mom. Monday isn't too early, either.

"There's a line when the door opens," says the owner's dad. Mom and Dad both help out at the restaurant.

"How much barbecue you at, Dad?" shouts Matt from across the kitchen. Matthew Register is the owner, and it's only noon. Dad is well past my age and chopping 'cue as if he's half my age.

Mom, meanwhile, is filling so many cups full of iced tea I'm surprised the tea hasn't run dry. Then somebody at the counter asks her for baked beans. "Sorry," she says. "Baked beans are off the board." Sold out.

But how? How could barbecue, beans, and tea run out at a well-run restaurant open just two days a week in a town of only 625 people? "It's fantabulous," says one of the locals. "Fan-tab-u-lous!" The man grips a bulky take-out box in each hand. He knew to call early.

"People said, 'You're opening this in Garland?'" I'm able to corral Matt for an interview. "But I had faith in how we were going to do it and what our product was." The main product is barbecue, and it seems the whole town is at the door. "If I was going to succeed or fail, why not do it at home?"

Matt grew up in Garland and opened Southern Smoke BBQ in 2014. But first, he practiced. "This is Jezebel," he says, introducing me to what looks like a huge hydrogen tank. "A member of the family." He raps the smooty smoker with his knuckles and tells me Jezebel helped him perfect his barbecue. His daughter helped him perfect his sauces.

"Oh, Dad, that's it, that's it!" his little taste tester said one day, and he agreed. And so he named the sauce for her: Sweet Grace. He named his other sauce Two Brothers. Grace has two brothers.

Matt has also experimented with his menu, which includes pork belly hash, bacon-and-white-wine cabbage, and tomato gazpacho. "We want to be something the people of Garland and Sampson County are proud of."

There's no seating inside the restaurant, so people sit outside, usually around a '56 Ford parked in back with a tabletop mounted over it and bars stools around it. "I just treasure old things like this," says a man with a spoonful of sweet corn near his mouth, a chrome fender by his knee and whitewall tire at his foot.

"Well, we just think it's marvelous," says an older gentleman who I learn is Matt's grandfather. He's dressed in coat and tie, and his wife wears a pretty dress.

"Wonderful," says Grandma. "I'm so proud of Matthew."

Although I'm rather anxious for Matthew. I hope he has enough food; his grandparents made a special trip. They're waiting now till the line subsides—which also makes me *glad* for Matthew. With a line like that, his grandparents have reason to be proud.

So do at least 625 other people.

LEFLER'S PLACE

6423 NC-73, MT. GILEAD, NC 27306, (910) 439-5451, LEFLERSPLACE.COM

It's the oldest operating cafe in Montgomery County—and the next county over, for that matter.

Lefler's opened in 1922, a cozy, two-room place that years ago was a gas station and then a grocery store. "Used to be everything," quips an old-timer.

The restaurant's grill is squeezed into a corner. "You don't have much room to work," I say to the cook.

"Yeah, and I'm big, too!"

The cook is Sam, a gray-haired fella who looks like he ought to be playing golf rather than flipping burgers. "Yeah, I'm retired now," he says and laughs; he's only kidding. Sam started working at Lefler's in 1959 and never stopped. "I came to work here when I was fifteen." For now, at least, he's retired from fixing breakfast for the day; he's at work on lunch, cooking burgers, hot dogs, and chicken.

"Homestyle, original, good," says one of the regulars. "They treat everybody like family."

It's a family cafe. Laura and Jimmy Anderson own it. Laura has blondish hair, a constant smile, and a "Hello" for everybody. "We're doing what God wants us to do," she says.

"It's really turned out to be a ministry," says Jimmy whose face is either naturally ruddy or he's just hot. He's in the smoky brick building out back, adding coals to the fire pit. Lefler's is well known for pit-cooked barbecue. "This is where the magic happens," he says, stoking the embers.

When not smoking barbecue—and chicken on Thursdays—Jimmy pastors a local church. "We have people come by all the time asking for prayer requests because they know I'm a pastor." He kindly offers encouragement—and feeds their souls.

Lefler's has long been a gathering spot in Mount Gilead. A hundred years of history. And now a ministry.

Laura makes the rounds, asking people how they're doing, how their kids are doing, how their meal is, and everyone returns her smile.

"It's a blessing," she tells me. "A blessing."

GENERAL MCARTHUR'S

13661 BARNES BRIDGE RD., LAURINBURG, NC 28352, (910) 276-1498

Old soldier's never die. They just fade away.
Old fishermen never die. They just smell that way.

I'm not sure who coined that second saying, but the first one belongs to Gen. Douglas McArthur who commanded troops in WWII and Korea. He was an intense leader, and yet I bet the general would have loved to sit a spell at the restaurant in Laurinburg that bears his name. But then, who doesn't like good fried chicken and barbecue?

Only the place isn't named after the general, not exactly, though the restaurant's logo hints at his likeness. The character in the logo wears a military uniform and flowing white bandana around his neck. He sports dark sunglasses and tucks a long corn cob pipe between his teeth—just like General McArthur; I've seen the wartime photos. Except the character in the logo is a pig—and I must say, the chubby little oinker is equally dashing.

I'm sure the restaurant means no disrespect to the late general. Actually, General McArthur and General McArthur's share a certain prestige, for the restaurant is also quite famous, or at least it is in its corner of the world in Scotland County.

Colin McArthur is the man who built the restaurant—no relation to General McArthur, as far as he knows. Colin is a tall man whose uniform is a ball cap and short-sleeve shirt open at the collar. "It just so happens it was a blessing in disguise," he says, meaning the restaurant and not the pig disguised as the general.

The dining area is big and barn-like with dark wood, overhead beams, and catchy signs hung here and there on the walls:

BARBECUE, I'M HOG WILD OVER YOU!

I'M SO FAR BEHIND I THOUGHT I WAS FIRST.

I STARTED WITH NOTHING. I STILL HAVE MOST OF IT LEFT.

Colin laughs at that last one. "That's me," he says.

He was raised on a Laurinburg farm and one day received a call from the army ordering him to Vietnam, but not on the front lines. "They called and told me I was gonna be in cook school." He, in turn, called his mom to tell her the news. "And all I could hear were my

sisters laughing in the background because I couldn't even boil water at the time."

The army taught him well. "We were feeding 350 people a day, and it really was a blessing because I never knew I enjoyed cooking so much."

When he returned home, he opened a catering business in Laurinburg and then built the restaurant. He built it out of two tenant houses that were on his farm. "Tenant houses?" I ask. Talk about a disguise; the building is impressive, and I never would have guessed. Maybe Colin and the general do share some history: mission accomplished in the face of staggering odds.

"Colin just oozes love and compassion for people, and you see that in his restaurant," says a middle-aged woman enjoying her lunch near a sign that reads LOVE SPOKEN HERE. "It's a magical story," she says.

And an impressive buffet: Barbecue, fried chicken, baked beans, black-eyed peas, macaroni . . .

"The love, fellowship and hospitality are what keep people coming here," a lady in line says. And by the looks of the delicious spread, the food keeps them coming, too.

I heap my plate and choose a table beneath another sign: SMILE. IT CONFUSES PEOPLE, which, of course, makes me smile.

The sporty little oinker with the corncob pipe does, too.

POSTSCRIPT

September 1, 2019, was a Sunday, and General McArthur's served four hundred people. Turkey and dressing were on special.

The restaurant closed at 5 p.m. By 6:30 p.m. it was all but destroyed.

Fire ripped through the building, an electrical fire that devoured the top half of the restaurant, which housed that handsome barn-like dining room. It was gone, and so was Colin McArthur's livelihood.

"It's a blessing," he says—not the loss, but the timing. Had the fire erupted sooner, the restaurant might have been full.

People from around the world immediately reached out. "From around the world," Colin says, amazed by the support. "A blessing," he says, and there's that term again, one he uses often.

As of this writing, Colin isn't sure what he's going to do. He thinks he can salvage the downstairs part, which housed the kitchen, and says he might reopen for catering only. Or maybe he'll rebuild, although he's in his seventies now and slowing down. But he keeps an upbeat attitude. "The sun will come up tomorrow," he says. "When one door closes, another opens."

Colin opened General McArthur's with the intention of creating a family restaurant, a place people thought of as truly special. It had been enjoying its best year in 2019, and Colin probably realized he'd attained his goal: a truly special place.

But it was after the fire when he became convinced, and therein lies the irony: knowledge gained in the face of loss. Such comfort despite such ruin.

"A blessing," he says once again. And there is irony in that, too.

MAMIE'S DRIVE IN

**9460 ANDREW JACKSON HWY., LAUREL HILL, NC 28351,
(910) 462-2130**

Fourteen stools, a walk-up counter and grill, that's it. Or is it?

"This place was surely God sent," says the cook. "I've had the opportunity to minister to a lot of folks." Maybe that's why people come, for the smile and encouraging word. And for the burgers, fries, and onion rings.

"Best onion rings around," says a lady in the parking lot on her way inside with her husband. "Amazing. We love Mamie's."

"Love it to death," her husband says. "Great hamburger, hot dog."

It must be great because the poster in the window declares it one of the top one hundred places to eat in North Carolina; the poster comes from an article out of *Our State* magazine, which is well-read and highly regarded.

"My favorite place," the husband says, shushing his wife toward the door. "We're starving," he admits. And maybe to appease his wife and make up for the shushing, he echoes what she said. "And the onion rings are really good."

The place is a simple, low, brick building off the highway in Laurel Hill, not far from Laurinburg or the South Carolina border. Step inside and up to the counter window where you'll be greeted by a friendly woman named Sheila. "I love it," she says. "We do everything fresh." She scribbles the next order. "Thank you, baby."

Mamie's opened around the late fifties, and Mamie sure was proud of Mamie's. "Little old lady who loved to please people," a longtime customer says. Mamie's picture hangs on the wall, a curly-headed woman with granny glasses and a gritty stare, eyes that I'm sure saw many a hard day's work. The new owners kept the name in tribute to her: Mamie's Drive In. They also stuck with her tradition of making everything fresh and homemade.

Back in the kitchen, a trio of pink-shirted cooks twirl this way and that so they don't bump into one another. I suppose they should be stressed over the lunchtime rush, but their tiptoe ballet has them smiling and laughing.

They gush over the Cheeseburger Challenge: double patties loaded with toppings, a doozy of a thing piled monstrously high. "It's, like, that tall," says one of the pink shirts, holding her hands to her chin. The challenge is to eat it in one sitting. "You should see their eyes bug out when they get it."

The Cheeseburger Challenge makes me think of the husband I interviewed earlier, a big man—and starving, too. I wonder if he accepted the challenge. I'd wager a basket of fries he did.

Though I bet his wife hoped he didn't. He wouldn't have room for the onion rings.

THE BERRY PATCH

**351 CARGO RD., ELLERBE, NC 28338, (910) 652-3276,
WORLDSLARGESTSTRAWBERRY.COM**

I like strawberries.

Cut them up, drop them in a bowl, sprinkle them with sugar, add milk. It's a good snack, or dessert. Healthy, too, and I don't mind using skim milk or sugar substitute. But given a choice, I think I'd pick blueberries instead and do the same. And yet, when I heard about the World's Largest Strawberry, well, it was no contest. I knew it was a story I had to do. And a berry I had to see.

The Berry Patch is off Highway 74 in Richmond County, and you can't miss it—even if you're on your way to pick blueberries. The World's Largest Strawberry is twenty-five feet high, eighty-six feet around, and houses an ice cream shop; inside the strawberry is strawberry ice cream, plus many other flavors, homemade and hand-churned. "The best ice cream there is," says a girl cranking the

machine. On busy weekends, as many as eight girls are cranking and scooping inside the giant strawberry.

"Does the World's Largest Strawberry sometimes feel too small?" I ask her.

"Definitely," she says. "We bump into each other all the time."

The strawberries themselves come from the owner's crops. "And we raise all types of produce, too," says Lee, the owner. He and his wife, Amy, run The Berry Patch, which is both an ice cream shop and produce stand.

"Cucumbers, squash, onions . . . " Amy begins ticking off the list. "Collards, cabbage, broccoli." She recalls how it all started. "We knew we needed to be unique." So she came up with an idea. A grandiose one.

"I said, 'You have lost your mind!'" Lee exclaims. He was flabbergasted when Amy pitched him her plan. And then he was intrigued. "How could I build a building like that? And I laid on the couch about an hour and a half, and I jumped up and said, 'I've got it figured out!'"

He built the World's Largest Strawberry out of wood and foam, which state bureaucrats soon wanted to trample. Engineers were reconfiguring the road and planned to plow right through the strawberry's center.

Lee was once again flabbergasted. And then intrigued. "I said, 'I believe I can pick this building up and move it.'" He propped it on a flatbed truck and hauled it a mile and a half down Highway 220.

"Terrifying," Amy says, though she can laugh now because the strawberry did not do a banana split. "Best thing we've done," she says, which I guess is why they often need eight girls dishing ice cream inside the strawberry.

"I can't help but think God had it all planned," Lee says, which is a good way to end my TV story on the World's Largest Strawberry. Except I've been saving two final questions. I know the answer to the first, but can't wait to capture the exchange on camera. "What's your last name?"

Lee smiles. "My last name is Berry, and people cannot believe it, but that's what it is."

Lee Berry, owner of The Berry Patch, builder of the World's Largest Strawberry—what a fun story. And now for the cherry on top: "What's your favorite ice cream?" I'm sure I know the answer to that one, too. But I don't.

"Butter pecan," he says.

SECOND STREET LUNCH

22 E. 2ND ST., ROANOKE RAPIDS, NC 27870

A little boy kicks a soccer ball. And the ball kicks back.

He's kicking it against a brick wall, which is part of a building, one that has stood for generations—and for who knows how many soccer-ball kicks. It's Second Street Lunch in Roanoke Rapids.

I want to ask the kid if I can try a few kicks, but I better head inside. The owners are expecting me—or at least I think they are. I couldn't call because they don't have a phone, so I rang town hall for help. The lady who answered was very nice. "Oh, yes," she said when I explained my predicament. She even volunteered to drive to the restaurant and tell them I'd be coming Friday. "I certainly will," she said. "You and your camera crew? My heavens. How exciting."

"Hamburgers and hot dogs," owner Greg Haislip tells me.

"I love a BLT and a grilled cheese," says his wife, Victoria.

They're behind the counter, Greg grilling, Victoria prepping. Greg is third generation; his granddad started Second Street in 1949. "I do the same thing Granddaddy did. We make the slaw the same way, the chili the same way."

"It's simple," Victoria says. "Cash only. No credit card machine, no phone. We're really old school."

They say keeping it simple means fewer distractions and more family time. Their family includes the towheaded soccer kicker who's just sidled up to the counter. "Fourth generation," Greg says.

I ask the whippersnapper if I can clip a mic to him, figuring he might as well get used to the spotlight if he's going to be a famous soccer star. Or maybe he'll own the restaurant one day. He agrees to the former, but not the latter. "Nah," he says when I power the mic and ask about running the place. "Too much work."

Mom and Dad throw up their hands and then get back to grilling and prepping. Orders are piling up, including a burger and fries for their little dynamo; kicking a soccer ball works up an appetite—especially versus a wall that always kicks back.

"So many people have grown up in Roanoke Rapids knowing Second Street Lunch," says a woman sharing a meal with her friend.

"It's the history," adds the friend. "And you can be yourself and enjoy talking and eating."

"I've been coming here since I was a little girl," says a mom at a table with her husband and teenage son.

"I've been eating here about twenty-five years myself," the husband says and rubs his belly.

They both mention the family atmosphere, and even the menu hints at family: The Club Laney and Sarah Ann Fries. Those are the owners' family members. I wonder about the Danny Boy on the menu and then meet Danny himself. Danny Haislip is second generation, Greg's dad, who ran the place for years until he retired. "I had a good time," he says. "International cuisine."

"International?" I say. "Hot dogs and hamburgers?"

He nods and tells me Second Street lunches have traveled the world. "Italy, Germany." He describes in detail how they're boxed and shipped and soon wins me over. And so does the Danny Boy, which includes the word "Triple" on the menu, written in parentheses. Must be a monster.

Another order for Greg and Victoria. I take a seat and watch them work and notice the occasional squeeze they give one another, a little hug here and there in passing, which warms my heart.

After a while, their little boy slides off his stool and trots outside again carrying the soccer ball. I want to tell him I'll be there in a sec and hope he lets me in on the game. I'll need to work off my Danny Boy.

And I'm sure that stubborn brick wall will help me do it.

BURGER BARN

328 E. MACON ST., WARRENTON, NC 27589, (252) 257-2368

Cheeseburgers, french fries, milkshakes.

Asparagus.

"Squash, green tomatoes, okra . . . " The chef lists the veggies he likes to use, while at the same time preparing something called the Big Eater Burger. "Two layers of meat, cheese, and bacon, and it's just amazing."

It's just a barn. Actually it's not even that, though that's part of the name. The Burger Barn used to be a Tastee Freeze back in the fifties, and old-timers in Warrenton still remember stepping up to the window for ice cream cones as kids. Now they order hot dogs and

sausage dogs, cheeseburgers and bologna burgers. Or the Big Eater with a side of okra.

"Good local produce," a lady in line tells me and says you never know what to expect, that the barn is more than just burgers, which makes it interesting. Others tell me it's also consistent.

"Quick sandwiches and great tasty food," says another woman waiting her turn at the window.

It's quite a mix at the Burger Barn. People park and walk up in everything from flip flops to loafers. A man in work boots throws me a wave. "Good place to be," he says.

"People come from all over," says an older man with a roly-poly stomach, his petite wife holding his arm, a sweet couple enjoying a lunch date. "They got great burgers," the man says, perhaps a bit too enthusiastically. His wife's polite smile slips, and she squeezes his arm. "And . . ." he stammers, "and, well, the chicken is to die for." Her smile returns.

They shuffle past me to the window, and I wonder if she'll let him indulge this time. I bet he'd love to dig into one of those great big Big Eaters. But no fries.

Asparagus instead.

GRANDPA'S KITCHEN

149 E. SOUTH MAIN ST., LITTLETON, NC 27850, (252) 586-3211, GRANDPASKITCHEN.ORG

They start singing soon after I walk in.

A table full of men who, spur-of-the-moment, break into song, a lively gospel tune. *"You are the Father,"* they sing, and their faces beam.

Grandpa's Kitchen is jumping the day of my visit. I'm not sure I've ever seen so many happy people inside a restaurant, this one a mom-and-pop—or a Grandma and Grandpa.

Jeff Mills and his wife, Johnell, own it. Jeff's mom makes the pies, and Johnell's mom makes the cakes. Jeff's sister is in charge of the barbecue sauce, and Johnell's aunt washes the chicken, and their children often pitch in, too, plus a niece and nephew. Everybody wears red T-shirts and big smiles, and what a busy kitchen: Grandpa's Kitchen where the whole family joins in, and where they cook the whole hog.

"Some of the best barbecue you'll find," says a contented customer.

"Barbecue chicken, that's my favorite," says another. "Makes you feel so wonderful when you come to this place."

"Yeah, we serve food, but we also serve love," Johnell says. She and Jeff grew up in Littleton, a small town in Warren County, not far from Lake

Gaston. They left to pursue careers—he became an engineer, she a biologist—but as time went on, they longed to return home.

"Back to Littleton?" I ask.

"There were no signs of life," Jeff says. "Nothing on this corner, but yeah."

They held fast to their faith and in 1997 opened Grandpa's Kitchen. "My driving force was the chicken," Jeff says. "If people could taste this chicken, I knew we were going to be in business."

Chicken slathered in homemade barbecue sauce; he's fixing some in the kitchen, and it looks fantastic, juicy and tender, and smells even better. Except my eyes keep drifting to the strawberry cake. "Made from scratch," Johnell says, while her mom finishes frosting it. "We're talking buttermilk, eggs, the whole shaboom."

A rhythmic shaboom is still going on around the table of men out front. They lift their voices and sway in unison, and what a profound show of fellowship. Clearly, Jeff and Johnell have succeeded in creating something special since taking their leap of faith.

You are the Father . . . !

AUNT MILLIE'S
PIZZA SUBS & SUDS

249 BROAD ST., MILTON, NC 27305, (336) 234-0240,
AUNTMILLIESPIZZA.COM

"Too big for one person to eat," says a teenaged girl.

The waitress has delivered a banana split, and the wide-eyed girl leans over it with a long spoon; the spoon hovers, and I don't think the girl knows just where to start. She shakes her head. "Nine scoops of ice cream," she says and at last digs in.

"Nine scoops," I murmur, peering over her shoulder. "Whoo." The thing is monstrous. "Gotta be bananas in there somewhere," I say.

"Oh, yeah," pipes the waitress—*You betchya*, she nods. "They're in there, alright." Then she nods at the bowl. *You'll see,* the nod says.

Sure enough, the spoon hits pay dirt. The girl pokes and prods and finally pulls, and out of the mountain emerges a hefty heap of ice cream, whipped cream, chocolate sauce, and—yes!—a chunk of banana barely visible beneath it all. The three of us stare, mouths open. The girl opens hers wider, and in goes the spoon, piled with a soft syrupy mountain slab. Her eyes grow even wider than her mouth. "Really good," she mumbles at last and reaches for a napkin.

Banana splits and pizza. Aunt Millie's is known for both. "Pound-and-a-half of cheese on it," the pizza maker says, topping the pie with pepperoni—*dozens* of slices of pepperoni. He tells me a large pizza weighs five pounds, and I can see why.

"It's funny when you hand it to somebody in a box," says Gwen McGuire, Aunt Millie's owner. She thrusts her body forward with a grunt, and the box she pretends to catch nearly knocks her off the stool.

Aunt Millie's itself probably catches people by surprise. The restaurant is in Milton, a dot of a town in Caswell County near the Virginia line. Downtown is a short but stately stretch with brick buildings and American flags, and which offers an inspiring footnote to history. For this is where Thomas Day built his prized furniture in the years before the Civil War. Day was a free black man and skilled carpenter whose workshop still stands and whose furniture is still sought after.

Aunt Millie's is no slouch for history, either. "The building's been here since the 1860s," Gwen says.

I can feel the history beneath my feet—the wooden floor creaks. The Guest Book up front is full of names from other countries even. But then, Virginia International Raceway is just a few miles up the road, and I gather race fans visiting from Australia and Egypt must also enjoy pizza and banana splits.

"Anybody who eats here and doesn't like it, something's wrong with 'em," says a crusty old-timer plopped at a picnic table on Aunt Millie's front porch. Though he sure is an enthusiastic fella. He slaps the table and raves over the pizza. "Amazin'." But when I ask about the banana split, he hesitates, then shoots a finger at me and asks if I've tried one.

"Well . . . "

The good-natured geezer cracks a mischievous smile and slaps the table again. "I'd like to see you after you eat one," he says. "I like to see people in misery."

TARHEEL BAR-B-Q

9 US-13, EURE, NC 27935, (252) 357-1094

Gates County is known for Merchants Mill Pond, a vast cypress swamp, worth the drive northeast for a getaway paddle, although you'll want to keep your eyes peeled for alligators . . . and save your belly for barbecue.

Tarheel Bar-B-Q is near the Mill Pond, a wide stretch of a building with a long overhang propped by a row of wooden posts, which gives the place a rustic cowboy kind of look despite the cars whizzing past on the highway.

The building seems like a throwback, and when I duck inside, the wall-to-wall wood paneling lends a comforting feel, as do the kindly folks who nod and smile.

"My dad started it in 1960," says owner Paige Hedgepeth. People called her dad Gramp and said he'd never make it, not in rural Gates County, and certainly not in a tiny town like Eure. *Eure not gonna make it*, they teased. She nods, brows arched above her eyeglasses, the look of a wise woman, Daddy's little girl.

Now, almost a half-century later, people routinely pull off the road, mosey in,

and grab a seat and a plate of barbecue. Or fried chicken and fish.

"Them corn herrings will slap your mama good," chuckles a man who tips his spotless dish at me. "Bones and all."

"Bones?" I say.

He tells me, yeah, bones, too. "Slap your mama."

I meet a man at another table who's 103 years old. "My father loves this place," says his son who's up in age himself. "His all-time favorite restaurant." I opt not to interview Dad, but not because of his frail frame. His mouth is full.

I ask Paige what makes the barbecue so special, and she tells me it's her daddy's secret sauce: sweet and spicy, and, of course, the more you use the tastier it gets.

The same can be said of the restaurant: The more ingredients you add, the more interesting the place becomes.

Silk scarves and handbags dangle on hooks along one wall and spill into an adjoining room. The other room is narrow, shaped like a corridor, and full of jewelry and clothes. "And we have the tanning beds," Paige says, gesturing to several small side rooms with full-length tubes arrayed with lights. Near the end of the corridor is a table where a young manicurist dabs pink polish onto a woman's nails.

"Make them nice and shiny," the manicurist says.

"Do you ever walk through the doorway and eat barbecue?" I ask her.

"Yeah, every day," she says, laughing—and I hope I haven't made her hand shake.

Paige says it's also the other way around: people eat first, then shop. And window shop.

She leads me to the corner of the restaurant and shows me a large plate-glass window with taxidermy displays mounted behind it. My eyes grow as big as the bear's. It's like a little museum with stuffed deer and a cougar and . . . I peer at a two-foot critter standing upright on two paws. An otter, I think, but in disguise. Someone has outfitted the furry fella with a straw hat and eyeglasses.

I congratulate Paige on everything she's done, a place to come get barbecue, chicken, and herring, along with clothes, a tan, and a manicure. And here in Eure.

Paige arches her eyebrows and turns her gaze toward her dad's framed picture on the wall. Gramp is nicely dressed in coat and tie with a trace of a smile. She smiles at the portrait as if to say, *Eure the best.*

EAST

SMITH'S RESTAURANT

3649 N. HALIFAX RD., ROCKY MOUNT, NC 27804, (252) 443-0418, SMITHSREDANDWHITE.COM/RESTAURANT

It's a restaurant and grocery store.

It may be the most famous grocery store in the state, and the restaurant is mighty popular, too. They go hand in hand, wall to wall, side by side. If the restaurant runs short of sausage, there's plenty more next door. "Yeah, right through the back," says the manager who may need a quick restock; the restaurant is buzzing and orders mounting. I've come at the day's busy intersection—breakfast and lunch, side by side.

"About 11:15, the breakfast crowd's letting out, and the lunch crowd's storming in," says a man who's long since claimed a table. He's with a group of other older men, and I'm pretty sure they're part of both crowds—their plates are clean, but their coffee cups are full. "The kinda food my mama made when I was growing up," the man quips, and the others chuckle. "I love Rocky Mount," he adds, and the others nod. "Been here fifty years."

The grocery store has been around even longer. Smith's Red & White opened in 1954, just a little building at a crossroads called Dortches on the outskirts of Rocky Mount. The store grew, and so did the area. Interstate 95 came in, and today travelers from across the country take the Dortches exit specifically to shop at Smith's, eager to snap up the store's world-famous sausage. At Christmastime, people bring their own coolers, bathtub-sized with plastic wheels, and load them up. No cooler? No problem. The store stocks plenty.

"I love this place," says a lady at the restaurant, snuggled in a booth, and I'm sure she means both the eating and shopping. She's a Rocky Mount native who says she witnessed the Red & White's growth. The store's popularity boomed so much that in 2006 the Smith family opened the restaurant. "Tenderloins, ribs, oysters, shrimp, corn, butterbeans." The woman is also plenty familiar with the menu. "And snap peas with a little ham hock. All that country cookin'. Always delicious."

And always a crowd. Interstate 95 never lets up.

I meet a family from northern Virginia on their way to south Florida who've stopped for lunch. "And the kids are saying how nice everybody is," remarks Dad. I can tell the youngsters are excited; they're bouncing in the booth. They say they've heard about the homemade cakes and old-fashioned candy next door.

The kids obviously can't wait to get to Disney World. But after lunch, they can't wait to go grocery shopping, either.

CENTRAL CAFE

132 S. CHURCH ST., ROCKY MOUNT, NC 27804, (252) 446-8568

Cotton, tobacco, railroads. They've all played a role in Rocky Mount's long history. So has Central Cafe.

It opened in 1927. The crops and trains faded over time. And Central Cafe has, too—which is part of the charm.

It may be the epitome of nothing fancy, not bright or sparkly or even cushiony. The hard, wooden booths aren't easy on the fanny, and yet folks have happily sat in them over the last century.

"I love the hot dogs, hamburgers, the whole works," says a man with salt-and-pepper whiskers who tells me he's been stopping in for a half century. He's a big man but looks rather comfortable in the booth; indeed, he talks at length about comfort, but he means the food.

The history counts for comfort, too. "Your whole heritage is in this place," I say to Keeling Hardy who's up to his wrists in hamburger meat, mixing it together in a bowl.

"I think it's great," he says and tells me he took over the place from his dad who took it over from *his* dad. "Consistency," he says, and I'm not sure if he means the restaurant or the meat. Maybe both.

I see a woman with two little girls in a booth, both girls with hair bows and hot dogs. "I have lived all over the world," Mom says, "and I can promise you that I have flown home strictly for a Central Cafe hot dog." Wow, that's a mighty bold statement, and I figure she must be exaggerating. "I promise you," she repeats, and she's adamant, though her girls don't flinch at Mom's stern tone. They're happily chomping, and I get the feeling flights home are in their futures, too. Airline tickets for Central Cafe hot dogs.

"Two all the way, extra mustard," I tell the girl at the counter and then carry them to a booth. The hard wood doesn't bother me. No cushion, no problem.

The dogs provide the comfort.

MEADOW VILLAGE RESTAURANT

7400 NC-50, BENSON, NC 27504, (919) 894-5430, MEADOWRESTAURANT.BIZ

Most Tar Heel Traveler restaurant stories are fun, the food good, atmosphere inviting, people friendly.

And that's how it was the day I stopped in at the Meadow Village Restaurant in Johnston County. "Country cookin'," said Julia Raynor who smiled and told me she opened the place with her husband in 1982.

She was sitting at a table, and people waved as they walked by or stopped to give her a hug and chat a minute. "Best restaurant I go to," one woman said to the camera, her arm draped around Julia's shoulder. Others offered the same sentiments.

"Oh, they have good fried chicken."

"The cooked apples are to die for."

"The desserts! They're the best."

Julia's daughter joined us at the table. "Good old-fashioned conversation," Sheila said. "I think that's why people like to come to Meadow."

I think people also enjoyed seeing Julia. "I've known her since I was a teenager," another woman said, addressing the lens, and it occurred to me people wanted to make sure their feelings were captured on camera—not for them, but for her, so that others would know Julia and how much she meant to the community. "She's a real trooper," the woman added and gave Julia's shoulder another squeeze. Julia tried to return the hug, but it was awkward being confined to a wheelchair.

I couldn't ignore it. Or the old news reports I'd read before my visit. I would love to have basked in the delicious buffet and focused my story on the food and all those fine people. The conversation was entertaining indeed, folks joking and laughing, but there was another story in front of me.

"I remember what happened right up until he hit me," Julia explained. It was difficult to ask her what happened but also necessary.

She was driving, alone in her SUV, when another car approached; as it turned out, one carrying a man, his girlfriend, and their four-year-old child. The couple was arguing; Julia found that out later. "And he told her he was going to kill them all, and he came across four lanes and hit me on purpose, intentionally."

Julia didn't shed any tears on camera, not even when she told me the crash broke every bone in her neck and paralyzed her

from the waist down. The family that hit her was not seriously injured; only Julia was. "It could have happened to anybody," she told me.

But it had happened to her, and Julia's family struggled with such cruel fate. "I have thoughts about it all the time," said her son, Timmy, who told me the man who'd hit her spent just twenty-four months in jail. "Probably walking the streets again," Timmy said and shook his head. "Whatever."

"I just try to take each day and make it the best I can," Julia said. Although I learned it was a rare day now visiting the restaurant she used to run every day. Transportation in a wheelchair made getting around difficult.

So her visit this day was a joyful surprise. "She has set an example for all of us," another friend said to the camera. "Don't let anything stop you or hold you back."

The hugs and waves went on, and so did the good conversation. The buffet remained full; the chocolate pies shimmered in the overhead light—oh, so chocolaty and moist.

And there was Julia, in the middle of all that warmth, surrounded by scrumptious food and genuine fellowship.

It was a good day indeed.

POSTSCRIPT

Julia Raynor died February 10, 2018, with her family by her side. She was seventy-eight years old.

Her death came three years after my visit to the Meadow Village Restaurant. *Village*—the word seems appropriate, the place routinely full of kind and neighborly folks.

That's what Julia established and what today continues. Though not there in person, she is present in spirit, and it's a joyous spirit in this happy, wholesome village.

It is Julia's lasting legacy.

THE BEEFMASTOR INN

2656 US-301, WILSON, NC 27893, (252) 237-7343

It's a restaurant without a menu.

"Just rib eye, baked potato, and salad bar," owner Chad Ellis says. He wears a visor on his head and a T-shirt, nothing fancy. And the restaurant isn't, either.

"No menu?" I ask.

"No menu!" he exclaims. It's an oddity but also the restaurant's claim to fame, that and the steaks. WORLD FAMOUS declares the slogan printed on Chad's Beefmastor T-shirt, the slogan stamped on a brown cow.

The restaurant is a small brick building along Highway 301 in Wilson. If you don't know to look for it, you might whiz right by and maybe opt for a burger at the drive-through down the road—and what a shame that would be.

Inside, the ceiling is low and the walls cinderblock, but the red-checked tablecloths add color. So do the rib eyes.

"Best steak I've ever eaten," says a man twirling a pink chunk with his fork. "Beautifully flavored with very little seasoning, and so tender."

"Just a little granulated garlic and salt," the chef says, sprinkling a rib eye he's added to the grill. He says he goes through about eight hundred pounds of meat a week and opens the fridge to show me his supply. The shelves are stacked with what look like fireplace logs, except they're maroon and coated in plastic. It's only Monday, and he's ready for the week ahead. The restaurant is open all seven nights. But then, it only has ten tables.

"Two- and three-hour wait sometimes," the prep cook tells me while chopping celery for the salad bar. She has already sliced tomatoes and filled bowls full of bacon bits and garbanzo beans. "But they don't mind waiting," she says. "They come here to wait."

People routinely bring lawn chairs and coolers full of beer and wine, and all of a sudden it's a tailgate party in the parking lot. "Like being at a football game, to be honest with you," Chad says.

I ask if he ever calls to folks outside, telling them their table's ready, and if they say, no, they want to wait some more. He laughs and nods. "Plenty of times."

The Beefmastor Inn opened in 1966. One man tells me he's been coming for fifty years. A husband and wife I interview, both graying at the temples, say it's their anniversary, and they wanted to celebrate at their favorite restaurant. "Always outstanding," the husband says.

"And I love the fact they bring the steak to your table and cut it to size," adds the wife.

Just then, the chef sidles up carrying a cutting board piled with a raw slab of meat. He carries the board with both hands and rests it at the table's edge. "I can start at eight ounces and go larger if you like," he tells the couple and hovers his knife over one end of the slab. They both say eight ounces is plenty, and he begins to cut. It doesn't take long; the blade is razor sharp. Then he excuses himself to prepare their order—but not without wishing them a happy anniversary.

I'm sure people at their tables don't mind waiting. No hurry on the rib eye, there's always the salad bar. I watch one man load his bowl nearly to overflowing, his face beaming. He tells me it's his first visit to the Beefmastor. "Reminds me of Steak and Ale, 1978," he says. '78 was thirty years before the Steak and Ale chain went bankrupt, back when times were simpler.

"Is there beauty in the simplicity?" I ask Chad.

"Yeah, 'cause we're not smart enough to serve all that other stuff," he says, laughing. "Just rib eye, baked potato, and salad bar"

"And no menu."

"No menu!"

PARKERS BARBECUE

2514 US-301, WILSON, NC 27893, (252) 237-0972,
PARKERSBARBECUEWILSON.COM

Twenty-thousand people a week eat at Parkers Barbecue. That's a lot of people.

"Been eating here since I was a little boy."

"Closest thing you'll get to Mama's."

"Best barbecue there is."

"A Wilson institution."

"A North Carolina institution."

It all began in 1946 with two brothers named Parker and a cousin who bought a piece of land along Highway 301, which, back then, was a major north-south link. "They built it, and all the neighbors helped build it," says Eric Lippard who today co-owns the restaurant with Kevin Lamm.

They sit for my interview, side by side in what look like school chairs from the fifties. In fact, the whole staff looks like they're out of the fifties, everyone dressed in crisp white shirts and many wearing white paper hats.

I ask Kevin and Eric about the restaurant's early days, which tickles them both; they laugh, and their chairs wobble. "What really put Parker's on the map was Purina Mills down the road," Eric says.

It was 1954, and Ralston Purina had just built a new plant in Wilson and decided to throw a party. The pet food company asked the

Parker boys if they could both host and cater it. "Sure," the Parkers said. But a party of seventeen thousand? Oh, boy!

The Parkers and staff got to work. They dug a long trench, strung hogs on wire, row after row of them, and smoked the pigs over the open pit below ground. They charged seventy-five cents a plate.

The pigs and party were a whopping success. Purina wrote the Parkers a hefty check, which is just what they needed. "They paid everybody they owed," Kevin says, "and the rest is history."

Lots of delicious history. The restaurant itself looks like an old schoolroom with simple wooden tables and chairs and wood paneling on the walls; not a one-room schoolhouse, but rather a long stretch of a place always full at lunch and dinner. "We cook between seven and eight thousand chickens a week," Kevin says. "About 150 whole pigs a week."

"And we sell a bunch of seafood," adds Eric.

"It's as busy now as it was then," says a longtime customer enjoying the last of his hush puppies. He says he remembers when 301 was a major thoroughfare. Today, it's more like a sleepy stretch, yet the slowdown apparently hasn't affected business. "It's as good as it was years ago," the long-timer says, and others agree.

"Like a down-home type place."

"They've never tried to pretty it up. It's just what it is."

"The best!"

Folks are bent over their barbecue, chicken, and seafood, and I hear them oohing and ahhing. I also witness quite a bit of hugging. "If you hug them, it sells a lot of barbecue, so we do a lot of hugging," Eric says with a laugh—and his chair wobbles. "The biggest reward is seeing it continue to grow and people telling us they've been eating here fifty years and that they believe it's as good or better than it's ever been. And that says a lot for a company that's more than seventy years old."

Twenty-thousand people a week says a lot, too.

FLO'S KITCHEN

1015 GOLDSBORO ST. S, WILSON, NC 27893, (252) 237-9146

"Cat head biscuits?" I ask.

The waitress nods. "Cat head biscuits!"

"Because they're as big as a cat's head?"

"Some are even bigger than a cat's head." The way she nods her blonde head has me convinced. The blonde head is serious about the cat head.

Flo's Kitchen is a tiny little place with a blue awning, known far and wide for its breakfast and biscuits. *"The Best 'Mouth Watering' Biscuits in Town,"* the menu proclaims.

"We put cheese in the biscuits," Linda Brewer says. She's the busy owner behind the counter. "Hoop cheese, big ol' cheese." She forms a wide circle with her hands. "Big ol' big biscuits." I notice she repeats the word "big."

Linda is as southern as they come. Every order she rings up and take-out bag she hands over comes with a, "Thank you, Sweetie. You have a good day now, Shug."

The Flo of Flo's Kitchen was Linda's mother, whose smiling face adorns the wall. "She died at eighty and was still making biscuits here when she died," Linda says, beaming at Mama's portrait.

The place Flo ran, and which Linda runs now, is about the size of a one-pump gas station, which it once was. "It was a gas station, a pool hall. It's 120 years old, this building is."

Six ladies are lined next to Linda, fixing biscuits, and I'm amazed at how they do it without bumping each other into the batter. "They're used to it," Linda says. "They all know how far they can go."

Flo's has just a handful of tables, and my buddy Keith has grabbed a seat. He writes for the local paper and knows the ins and outs around Wilson. "I usually get the tenderloin biscuit," he says just as the blonde waitress slides him his plate; she throws me another nod that says, *Told ya'. Big as a cat's head.*

Keith wedges both hands under the biscuit and lifts it gently; he even displays it for me, twirling it front and back as though it were a bar of gold—it might just be heavier. "This biscuit's the size of three biscuits most places," he says and seems so thrilled I think he hates to take a bite—it's so big he might be better to start with a nibble.

"Oh, Lord, they're huge!" cries a man who's just slid into a booth. "Can't eat more than one!" He roars with laughter and slaps the table as if to say, *Bring it on!*

I take in the crowd and notice the staff lady at the drive-through leaning in and out of the window as if on a seesaw—and at the moment, she's on the downswing. "Got you an egg biscuit. Thank you, Sweetie." She hands the bag to the driver, then catapults inside again where she stuffs another bag. I walk over and ask how long the line gets, hoping I don't throw a wrench in her rhythm. "Can be a block away," she says, and down she goes. "You have a good day now, Honey."

I wander outside, and the line *is* a block long, a mid-morning traffic jam on Goldsboro Street. But they've got to be the happiest bumper-to-bumper drivers I've ever seen. "The best restaurant in the south," declares a truck driver in a neon vest who says he stops by every day—and every day it's stop and go.

"Just handmade, homemade," squeals a lady, squirming behind the wheel. "Just, just . . . " She's so squirmy and excited she can't seem to find the right words—I just hope she keeps finding the brake. "Like straight from the kitchen," she finally blurts, and the line finally crawls.

Time for my own cat head, and I start back inside, hoping Keith has saved me a seat, although by now he's probably finished eating. I bet Linda is giving him a "Thank you, Shug" at the counter right about now.

Or maybe he *is* still eating; after all that tenderloin biscuit of his was, well . . .

Bigger than a cat's head.

WILSON DOUGHNUT SHOP

525 TARBORO ST., SW, WILSON, NC 27893, (252) 243-5325

A doughnut cake nearly half a foot high. Great mountain of glazed magnificence!

A young couple has ordered it and now they gawk at it. It's been brought to their table, a kind of lopsided pyramid, doughnuts piled one on top of another, a dozen or more; it's hard to tell how many because of all the icing. I'm not sure the couple knows where to begin.

"I think everybody knows," says a Wilson Doughnut Shop regular, though he's not talking about the doughnut cake. "I think everybody knows about the doughnut shop." It's a Wilson landmark, he says, and tells me he rarely skips a day, which surprises me—he's skinny. I figure he comes for coffee and fellowship, no doughnut cake for him.

Vera Beamon used to be a regular, too, a petite woman with short blonde hair and glasses, once a customer, now the owner. "Oh, I've loved it," she says. "It's been great."

She's convinced it was also fate.

"It was a prayer she had," says her husband, Doug. "That's really what happened."

Vera had been searching for a job. She didn't know what job, just that she longed to get out, be productive, and spread some joy. She always felt happy on her frequent visits to the doughnut shop; it was just that kind of place, she says, and she began to think, *What if?*

"We asked the Lord to bless her with the doughnut shop," Doug says, and one day Vera and Doug approached the man who owned it. "And he said he'd been praying for God to send him somebody to buy it, somebody who'd take care of it because he cared about it." It was an answered prayer—actually, three of them: Vera's, Doug's, and the man's.

The Wilson Doughnut Shop opened in 1952, a humble place trimmed in green. "Excellent," exclaims a man with a clean plate and frosted fingers. "Five stars in every category." Especially the

sweetness category, although it also serves bacon and eggs and hot dogs and hamburgers. "People have heard of the doughnut shop from counties away," the man says. "It's got a super reputation. A real anchor for the Wilson community."

Anchor seems apt. Eat one of those doughnut cakes in one sitting and you'll no doubt be anchored to the couch when you get home.

But *anchor* is appropriate for another reason, Vera and Doug are anchored in their faith. "Do you feel you were led here?" I ask.

Vera has just begun to box a rack full of strawberry doughnuts. "Yeah," she says. "I do," and the way she says it—her soft but steady voice, gentle smile, and kind eyes—exudes gratitude and happiness.

The strawberry doughnuts exude happiness and sweetness.

DICK'S HOT DOG STAND

1500 NASH ST. N, WILSON, NC 27893, (252) 243-6313,
DICKSHOTDOGSTAND.COM

He called me two weeks before he died.

I was on a story and couldn't talk long, but it was great to hear from Lee—though a bit unusual for him to be calling. I was surprised he had my cell number; I must have left it with him all those years before.

It was 2008 when I first met Lee Gliarmis at his restaurant in Wilson: Dick's Hot Dog Stand, open since 1921, and much more than just a stand. It is a cozy, crowded place with apple-green booth cushions and old pictures cluttering the walls. I lost myself looking at them, spotting Andy Griffith, Clint Eastwood, Burt Reynolds, and Angela Lansbury. And then all the sports photos, especially baseball: Babe Ruth wearing pinstripes and a gap-toothed grin.

Lee chatted behind me as I peered, telling me of his long love for baseball and athletics in general. He'd played three sports as a student at UNC and dreamed of a career as a coach. But then his brother was killed at the Battle of the Bulge, and there was the restaurant to look after, the family business.

He tapped a finger on a pen-and-pencil sketch of a bespectacled man with a mustache and receding hairline: his dad, he explained, who'd come from Greece and settled in Wilson with dreams of his own. His name was Socrates "Dick" Gliarmis.

"This community has been great to my family and the business," Lee said, and I could tell how deeply he meant it. By this time, we'd sat down and he tilted the bill of his ball cap back. His brown eyes

gleamed with a gentle but determined stare, and he rested his arms on the table and leaned toward me. "Eighty-seven years. That's hard to beat."

The restaurant was celebrating its eighty-seventh anniversary back then, in 2008, a dream more than fulfilled.

"Oh, you couldn't ask for a nicer place," a man with two hot dogs told me. "Best hot dog I've ever eaten." He'd ordered his smothered with chili.

"Just feels like home," said a woman in a booth with her friend.

"Very comfortable," said the other woman—except on Sundays after church, she added. "There's a mad rush from the Methodists to get here before the Episcopalians." Both women reared back, laughing.

"It means a lot to Wilson," another customer told me. Although he didn't have to tell me because it seemed obvious. Maybe it was all those nostalgic photos, the smiles on the walls—and at the tables. Or the food, simple comfort food: American with Greek influence, a rich Greek heritage Wilson had both respected and admired.

Dick's Hot Dog Stand was approaching its one-hundred-year anniversary the day Lee called my cell in early March 2019. I'd kept in touch with him over the years and had even signed books at his restaurant. I had a new book coming out, and he invited me for another signing. I suppose that's why he called, though we also chatted about Fleming Stadium. He'd led the effort to renovate the town's historic ball field, which included the North Carolina Baseball Museum, a brick building in the shadow of the third-base line. I'd done a story on it in the past, and Lee told me of all the mementos that had been added since.

Maybe the museum is why he called, that and the future book signing; I'm not sure but it was good talking to Lee. It would be the last time.

He died March 14, 2019, at ninety-one years old. His wife had passed away just five weeks earlier; they had been married sixty-two years. One of the news articles quoted a longtime friend who said they were meant to be together—and still are.

Today, Dick's Hot Dog Stand still serves hot dogs and continues a tradition it started in 1921, and for that Lee would no doubt be grateful and proud, and I'm certain his dad would be, too. I'm sure they would also be humble. Even the name of the restaurant is humble: Dick's Hot Dog Stand.

But it is so much more than a stand.

WHOLE TRUTH LUNCHROOM

515 WALNUT ST. S, WILSON, NC 27893, (252) 237-5595

Fried chicken, baked chicken, pork chops, mac 'n cheese . . . That's some good eating. And that's the truth, the whole truth, and nothing but the truth.

"Soul food!" proclaims a man with a bag full of to-go boxes.

The soul of the Whole Truth Lunchroom in Wilson is the church next door. The two brick buildings sit side by side. "It started off with feeding the church members," says a longtime parishioner who's also a Lunchroom cook. She says it all began more than sixty years ago and that the church members loved the food so much, word soon spread. "And the outside people wanted to be accommodated." In other words, people in town wanted some of that good fried chicken, too!

"Cooked with perfection and love," says a woman in line. "And you can feel the warmth when you come into this restaurant." She's a soft-spoken woman who seems quite sincere; I think she means what she says, and what she means is that the place is more than just a lunchroom. In many ways it's a mission, for the profits from the restaurant help sustain the church. The woman talks about food, faith, and fellowship—together under one roof.

The line to order grows long, and people can hardly wait. They chat about the famous chicken and how cheesy the mac 'n cheese is, and they tell me I need to come on a Friday because that's fish day, and the boneless trout is out of this world. They talk of the hush puppies, bread pudding, and sweet potato pie.

I maneuver my way to the kitchen and find the fried-chicken cook who greets me with a pleasant smile and dozens of crispy pieces she's collected in a wire basket; she holds the basket up for me to see. "One of the best chickens in the nation," she says. "We're ranked in the top fifty."

"Top fifty in America?" I say. "For chicken?" She nods and mentions a magazine that did the ranking; she can't remember the magazine but definitely remembers the ranking.

"Top fifty."

I ask her about neck bones, which I see are also part of the menu. "Neck bones?"

"Oh, they're very popular," she says. "We cook them in gravy." She says she often eats them herself. "You know, I used to be skinny when I first came here." She laughs, and I figure she's kidding—she *is* skinny.

"I'm working in the Lord's kitchen," she says, and her smile is as wide and pleasant as ever, and this time I know she's telling the truth. The whole truth.

BILL'S GRILL

5615 US-117 ALTERNATE, WILSON, NC 27893, (252) 239-1627;
119 NASH ST. W, WILSON, NC 27893, (252) 243-9003,
BILLSGRILLNC.COM

It's cold and rainy the day I arrive, but the crowd inside is all smiles.

Bill's Grill is a happy-busy little place in Wilson County, near the Black Creek community. "Today I got the pimento cheese bacon burger," says a burly man in a booth. "Excellent!"

In another booth are a husband and wife who say they come to Bill's Grill every Monday. Somebody else tells me Tuesday is chicken pastry day and Wednesday is great for spaghetti and chicken parmesan.

"On Thursday night he has a rib eye steak that is out of this world," pipes a man at the counter.

"And they're famous for seafood on Friday night," says a woman at a table. "Shrimp and trout."

I admire the young owner; I think Will Jenkins has the biggest smile of all. He's in his early thirties, and while chopping his spatula on the grill tells me about his cheesesteaks and hamburger steaks, pork chops and chicken wings. He took over the restaurant from his dad who opened the place in 1974, then

opened a second location in downtown Wilson. "I love what I do," he says. "Great customers, great staff, family environment. You know everybody by name."

A waitress makes sure I don't forget about dessert. "Our Oreo dirt cake," she says, flashing her big brown eyes and digging a spoon into a tin full of chocolaty-vanilla crunchies.

I'm surprised Bill's has a drive-through—it doesn't seem like a drive-through kind of place—but I watch the brown-eyed waitress bag up an order, lean out the little window and hand lunch to a woman behind the wheel. The woman smiles and says thank you before driving off.

Too bad, I think, certain the lady's smile must already be slipping away. Had she come in and sit a spell, she'd no doubt be smiling still. And maybe enjoying a cheeseburger with onion rings piled on top— the waitress tells me that's her favorite.

"The best," she says, flashing her big brown eyes.

B'S BARBECUE

751 B'S BARBECUE RD., GREENVILLE, NC 27858, (252) 758-7126

"It's the best barbecue in Pitt County," the lawyer tells me.

He's on his lunch break—and so is his sport coat; it's nowhere in sight. His tie, meanwhile, lollygags around his neck.

"Best barbecue in Pitt County?" I ask, egging him on. I've heard a lot about the place, and I guess he has, too. Itty bits of pig are snuggled in his mustache.

"It may be the best barbecue in the whole world." *Attaboy!*

B's Barbecue is not much bigger than my backyard shed—an unflattering comparison, I suppose, given the condition of my shed; it's old and leaky and about to fall over. I get dizzy rummaging for a nut and bolt because the floor slants.

B's is a rickety box of a building with a walk-up window outside and a bulky fan jammed in another window, blades thumbing, panes rattling. It's hard to believe the place is a restaurant. It actually looks like an old tool shed. I'm not sure if the floor slants, but I do feel dizzy inside—from a tangle of smells colliding between the paneled walls: barbecue, chicken, sauce, sweat.

It's hot inside; there's no air conditioning and it's jam-packed, and it's not even noon yet on a weekday. I ask a sweaty-faced woman carrying take-out if it's always like this. "Oh, my God," she pants. "You gotta spend the night to get some chicken." She laughs; she's joking, but it's probably not far from the truth. She hefts two bulging bags in each hand, grips them by their plastic straps. She's a small woman, and the load threatens to yank her arms to the floor—and maybe the floor *is* slanted. She waddles past me in a seesaw lumber, grunting for the door. She's come early and has stocked up—and I think she'll sleep well tonight.

"Almost outta chicken!" a woman in a purple T-shirt shouts from behind the counter. She lifts one aluminum lid after another. "Well, I am outta chicken," she says, though she doesn't seem flustered—I get the feeling she's used to it. But then she lifts the biggest lid of all, and her face beams. The tin still brims with chopped barbecue.

Tammy Godley is her name, her purple T-shirt emblazoned with *East Carolina University*. She's the owner and tells me all about her daddy who opened B's in 1978. "Just on a whim, and we been going ever since."

She shows me a grainy picture of her daddy who has long since passed away. He's seated in a chair, surrounded by his daughters, a shy smile beneath his dark mustache.

"Does this place still have his personality?"

"Yes, he's here every day, even though he's not."

I ask Tammy if the legend is true. "Once you sell all the barbecue, you close the door?"

"That's it," she says and tells me they've been known to close by noon on game days. On a football Saturday, B's might cook as many as twelve pigs, slow cooked all night long. And the barbecue goes fast.

"The best," exclaims a man in a wooden booth. "Eastern North Carolina barbecue," he says and shakes his bald head. "Hmm, hmm. There's no barbecue like B's. It's number one." He points his index finger toward the ceiling, which might be slanted, too.

The clock drifts past noon, the crowd swells, and the temperature inside rises. But I don't mind; it's all part of the experience.

Tammy plants her fists on her hips and looks around. I look, too, and think of my backyard shed. I guess I could build a fancy new one, but it wouldn't be the same; I like my decrepit shed.

"Means a lot," Tammy says. "Means a lot to all of us, and we're very proud."

Very hungry—yes, I am. *Dizzy* with hunger. I better order quick.

Before they close the door.

BUD'S GRILL

1601 N. MAIN ST., TARBORO, NC 27886, (252) 823-5665

It's called Bud's, but Sheila Mae steals the show.

She's a squinter; she squints when she smiles, and she squints a lot, even when writing down orders—she writes a bunch.

Sheila Mae must be my age, and, yes, we both share a few creasy lines, though I can't tell if any of hers zigzag across her forehead. She wears a red hat pulled low with "Bud's Grill" and a smiley cheeseburger face embroidered above the bill. Her reddish hair wisps about her ears.

But it's not Sheila Mae's squint, smile, or hair that's so distinct. It's her voice: southern smoky and as course as sandpaper; it's like a heavy-metal rift with genuine melody, it's interesting to listen to. It's . . . oh, my gosh . . . it's Janis Joplin, the sixties hippy rocker, voice reincarnated.

I order a pizza burger—reluctantly. To me, pizza is pizza, burgers are burgers, no crossovers allowed. But everybody, it seems, orders pizza burgers when they come to Bud's. So when in Rome . . . Well, at least my lunch will be half-Italian.

There's a bunch of burgers on the grill already, and I watch the cook spoon them with tomato sauce and pile mountains of shredded cheese on top, which sets off a mini avalanche; stray shreds tumble and topple onto the grill. *SSSSS!* The hiss, the cheese, the burger, the sauce. *Sheila Mae!* I want to holler. *Make that two!* Man, oh man, I've become a crossover convert even before my first bite.

"If it wasn't great, I wouldn't be standing here talking to you. I'd be somewhere else eating," says a Bud's fan, and I like that, a customer who tells it like it is.

So does Sheila Mae. "Best hot dogs in town," she says. "We got *the best* hot dogs."

Bud's is equally known for Buicks and Baracudas. Pictures of old cars dangle from the walls and are even painted on the side of the building, a colorful mural alive with fifties and sixties classics. The bright yellow, black-topped Baracuda belongs to Bud. The mural captures reality.

Bud's name is printed in white letters on the red awning out front, and yet here he is, the owner, inside sweeping the floor. He's older than I am, short hair, round face, and an easy smile. "You look around, everybody's laughing, having a great time," he says, then goes back to sweeping and greeting, a warm hello to everyone who walks in.

"It's a gathering place for all those people who used to work at Taicaro and Dixie Yarn and Pillowtex," a man informs me. He's one of the regulars, he says. He's in jeans and a leather jacket and says Bud's is more than just a little corner diner, that it actually stands as a symbol of hope for the town of Tarboro. "A beacon," he says. "Good food and fellowship."

Bud himself labored for years at a textile plant until it closed, which must have been a punch in the gut. But he picked himself up, opened a door, and welcomed folks in.

"You know, you think of fast food restaurants, you think about going in, getting your food and leaving," Bud says, still gripping the broom handle. "But we have people eat up here all day."

It's a small place with a few scattered tables but dominated by a long counter. The stools are full, and so is the grill. *SSSSS!* Pizza burgers and hot dogs.

"We got the best hot dogs because we got homemade chili," Sheila Mae says in that smoky-, southern-, sandpapery voice, and, gosh, I think I could sit here all day myself and eat. And listen to Sheila Mae. Pizza burgers and hot dogs.

And Janis Joplin, voice reincarnated.

ON THE SQUARE

115 E. JAMES ST., TARBORO, NC 27886, (252) 823-8268

You cannot change the painful past. Perhaps all you can do is savor the present.

I watch her sip red wine. She sits alone in a booth and gently tips the glass, and when those few delicate ounces touch her tongue, she closes her eyes and for a moment seems completely lost in herself.

She savors the wine; I know because I also watch her throat, and her Adam's apple does not move. Neither do I.

I eavesdrop on her private moment and can almost taste the wine myself. I swallow hard. She doesn't swallow at all for a full five seconds.

Inez is her name, and wine is her career. She grew up in Tarboro, graduated from UNC, and worked in restaurants from a young age. "Pizza Inn," she tells me later and laughs.

In time, she worked her way up to the largest grossing restaurant in North America—and it was a long way up indeed. Inez was a wine connoisseur for Windows on the World, the world-famous restaurant on the 107th floor of Tower One of the World Trade Center.

She was not there on September 11, 2001.

"My sister had gotten married on the eighth of September, so I was home in Tarboro."

But her husband was still in Manhattan. Stephen was a chef at Windows on the World and was due at work that morning at 11. "So I got up around 9:45, and my answering machine had twenty-seven messages."

They both lost friends and co-workers. "You see these people every day, and then all of a sudden they're gone," Inez says. "Permanently gone."

She and Stephen tried to start over in New York after September 11. "But it wasn't the same," she says. "We didn't make it past April."

So they escaped to her hometown and bought a run-down luncheonette, overhauling it and bringing fine wine and high-end dining to Tarboro. "We started doing small plates," Stephen says. "Tapas, which her father thought was topless, thought we were trying to get strippers. He's like, 'I don't know if topless will work in Tarboro."

The three of us enjoy a good laugh. And it's good to see them laugh. Of course, September 11 is in the distant past. And yet, not so

far away. "It changed my perspective on life," Stephen says. "Life is too short. I appreciate things a little bit more now."

He shows me the kitchen, talks of using local produce and lists some of his specialties: lamb, duck, quail. "I love fresh fish," he says and then begins making a cantaloupe, blueberry, and watermelon salad.

On the Square also offers a vast wine selection, thanks to his wife's expertise. Inez tells me how happy she is being home in Tarboro. It had been a risk opening such a restaurant in town, but it's now drawing people from across the state and beyond. And keeping her busy. She slips away to tend to something, while I admire the airy, elegant décor and scribble notes.

And a short time later, everything stops.

I hope she doesn't mind me watching as she sits alone in a booth and tips her glass and draws that delicate sip. Perhaps she's merely weighing whether to add that particular wine to her selection. Her eyes remain shut as mine absorb her absorbing the moment.

She savors the wine. And the moment, too.

THE SKYLIGHT INN

4618 S. LEE ST., AYDEN, NC 28513, (252) 746-4113, SKYLIGHTINNBBQ.COM

He grips a machete in each hand.

Well, they're not machetes exactly, but I'm sure each could fell a dense tree limb in a single swoop. *Swoop, swoop.* Except the muscle man works them more like drumsticks. *Chop, chop.* He pounds with both hands at the same time.

Chopper is his name, and it's also the name of his knives: Chopper 1 and Chopper 2. "My boys," he says and twirls them like pistols around his trigger fingers, then flips them in the air. The boys perform synchronized somersaults, doubly impressive when the overhead fluorescent ricochets off the steel blades. Chopper 1 and 2 flip twice before their handles fall squarely back into Chopper's firm grip: safe, sound, snug, and ready for work.

Chopper the muscle man is a tall man, all arms in a tight-fitting T-shirt—the shirt's backside reads, MORE THAN A GOOD BUTT. On the table in front of him is a cutting board, which he towers over and powers over, chopping barbecue slabs into minced meat, thanks to his boys.

But then somebody interrupts, a man in a streaky apron clutching a wobbly platter with a fresh hunk of hog. Streaky Apron Man tilts the tray, shakes it hard, and the hunk *thunks* onto Chopper's messy board. And the boys . . . Oh, they're like sharks sniffing blood. They twitch and tap, *tap-tap* the board's edge. Chopper, meanwhile, eyes the prize and flashes a wicked smile; his wild eyes and big teeth are as menacing as his "machetes." Then it's the pistol twirl again and— *Bang, bang! Chop, chop!*

"Best barbecue anywhere."

"Best I ever eat."

"Best ever."

Best is the word of the day. One after another, people exclaim over the 'cue, and the people exclaiming include the owner. "I think we do a heck of a job," Sam Jones says. His granddad, Pete, opened Skylight Inn in 1947. "It put Ayden on the map."

Ayden is in Pitt County, south of Greenville, north of Tick Bite—I can't wait to visit Tick Bite. The barbecue at Skylight Inn is whole hog, slow cooked over hot coals.

"There's nothing that takes the place of cooking with wood," Sam says and shows me the hickory pile out by the parking lot. It's so big that when he wanders to the other side, I can barely see the top of his head.

"Does it make a difference cooking with wood?" I shout.

"It's a flavor you don't forget."

The Skylight Inn is a past winner of the James Beard Award, which is like a culinary Oscar, but it doesn't display a shiny gold statue—although it does show off plenty of silver. The restaurant's roof is topped with a large statuesque silver dome, like something you might see on a state capital building. The silver is part of Skylight's signature, and regulars claim the inn is right to wear such a crown, that it is truly a barbecue king.

"If it's not from Skylight Inn, it just ain't cooked at all," a man who has just arrived tells me. He looks up, admiring the dome before entering to order his meal.

If he orders barbecue, and I'm sure he will, it will contain bits of skin from the hog. Chopper chops that, too—the *cracklings*, people call it. "Crunchy," a fella at a table says. "It's like a surprise in the barbecue. It's delicious."

But I wonder if Chopper and the boys think it's disappointing. I can't imagine chopping skin requires much muscle, even if it's cooked and crispy.

Ahh, but there's Streaky Apron Man again, rounding the kitchen corner now with another loaded platter. Chopper's eyes spring wide, and his big teeth gleam—the boys gleam, too. He twirls the twins around his trigger fingers and flips Chopper 1 and 2 in the air, then catches them in his mitts, and . . .

Bang, bang! Chop, chop!

SIMPLY NATURAL CREAMERY

**1265 CARSON EDWARDS RD., AYDEN, NC 28513, (252) 746-3334,
SIMPLYNATURALCREAMERY.COM**

Cow Pattie ice cream?

"Delicious," says the young server behind the counter.

Well, at least the name is spelled with an ie—Cow Pattie instead of Patty—but still, in my mind it conjures an image opposite of delicious. "Some of the best ice cream I've ever eaten," the server says, and the kid means it; either that, or he's nudging me to hurry up and order. Forty flavors on the board, and he insists Cow Pattie is his all-time fave and tells me it's chocolate ice cream with bits of peanut butter. "Delicious," he says again. "Cow Pattie."

Simply Natural Creamery is known for ice cream *and* cows. Neil Moye shows me the Jersey cows that graze his property. His dairy farm includes the ice cream shop, but the cows came first. He raises more than 150 head on his Greene County land, grass-fed cows. "All natural," Neil says. "Very efficient."

He introduces me to his wife, Jackie. They're both younger than I am but have already been married twenty-five years, and the Ayden area has long been their home. They seem happy, and the cows do, too; they're better groomed than my dogs, tan in color, big but lean, and often swish their tales. The Jerseys are productive; Neil also sells milk.

"Whole milk, low fat, skim," he tells me as we walk through the production building and by lots of stainless-steel tubing. "And this is actually where the cream is separated."

And where the cream eventually becomes ice cream. Back in the shop, a woman at a table with a hefty scoop on her spoon says, "Yeah, you get to see the cows that produce the milk to make the ice cream."

The shop's many flavors include Strawberry and Blueberry Cheesecake, Apple Dapple, Cinnamon Bun, and Salty Caramel, plus Cow Tracks and Moo-Moo Hugs. The creamery also makes its own cones, using a gadget that rolls flat waffles into cylinder shapes, which for me seals the deal. I've made one decision anyway: waffle cone instead of a cake cone.

The server behind the counter shuffles his feet. People are beginning to line up behind me, so I throw caution to the cows and place my order.

And I must say, I gotta give the kid credit, he's right, it's delicious. Cow Pattie.

MICKEY'S PASTRY SHOP

2704 GRAVES DR., GOLDSBORO, NC 27534, (919) 759-4741, MICKEYSPASTRY.COM

Doughnuts covered in chocolate. Shirts covered in stripes.

Mickey McClenny was a college football referee, an Atlantic Coast Conference head linesman. "He almost went to the NFL," his daughter Carole tells me. Mickey himself was busy with the doughnut shop; he had to officiate that instead.

Mickey worked for a candy maker as a kid and as a pastry chef during World War II. He fed the troops, and when he returned home in 1946, he bought a bakery in downtown Goldsboro and called it Mickey's Pastry Shop.

Mickey invented many of his own recipes, and for the next half century sold deliciously sweet goodies, while also working his way up the football chain.

"The NFL?" I ask, and Carole nods. Yes, he was that good. But so were his baked goods, she says, and he just couldn't leave the shop.

The pastry shop also became a way of life for Carole. She grew up with her dad's cakes and cupcakes and later married a boy named Jerry who hired on at the bakery. Jerry learned from Mickey, and in time they both became certified master chefs.

Meanwhile, Jerry and Carole were raising a family, and today their son and daughter both work at the pastry shop; in fact, daughter Melanie is a certified master baker herself. In 2003 she became the first third-generation certified master baker in the country and also the youngest.

Melanie was in her mid-thirties when I meet her in 2015, dark hair beneath a pastry-shop cap, a trace of flour on her green chef's jacket. "There aren't many bakeries in the country that have three certified master bakers, two of which are still working every day," she says. She includes Mickey as number three, though he died in 1999.

"Do you think about your granddad?"

"Oh, every day."

The shop still uses his recipes and even some of his 1940s equipment. Melanie's brother, Jerald, is in back, operating a machine that turns out long johns on a conveyer belt: plump, bar-shaped pastries full of cream. "It'll spit out sixty a minute," Jerald says over the rumble.

The long johns and other pastries are shipped across eastern North Carolina. "Everything made from scratch," Melanie says.

Mickey would no doubt be proud knowing the pastry shop is still thriving, yet I can't help but wonder about his head linesman career and his chance at refereeing in the NFL. "He knew his business meant a lot to our community," Melanie says. "He wanted to keep it going."

And so it has. Since 1946.

The place is full of school children the afternoon I visit. "They're piling in," Jerry cries, and everywhere I look I see happy, messy faces. The kids are loving the doughnuts—the moms are scrambling for napkins.

"Just a lot of fun," adds Carole.

"I wait on generations of customers every day," Melanie says. "Generations."

CHEF & THE FARMER

120 W. GORDON ST., KINSTON, NC 28501, (252) 208-2433, VIVIANHOWARD.COM

I'd heard so much about the Chef & The Farmer before I arrived. And not just heard, but seen.

I'd seen owner Vivian Howard host *A Chef's Life* on Public TV, syndicated nationwide, and much of it filmed at the restaurant. Plus, it seemed like every time I opened a magazine at the dentist office or barber shop, there she was, Vivian and one of her signature dishes splashed across two full pages.

But a top-of-the-line restaurant in Kinston?

In my early days as the Tar Heel Traveler I visited Kinston for a ghost story. It was 2008, and the town was all but dead—well, except for a pesky corpse that people swore haunted a local house. After covering the story, I felt sure any future trips to Kinston would be few and far between, though not because of the ghost, which was a lively little thing. Paranormal experts kept hearing doors slam and mysterious chatter. But otherwise, the town seemed hauntingly quiet.

And then along came Vivian.

"My husband Ben and I were working for some of the best chefs in New York City," she says in the TV show's voice-over intro. But then her parents back home in Kinston pitched an intriguing idea. They'd put up some of the money if Vivian and Ben opened a restaurant in North Carolina. "So we thought, 'Okay,'" Vivian recalls. "'Great, I'd love to open a restaurant in Asheville.'"

"There was a catch," the TV voice-over says. *"We had to open this restaurant in eastern North Carolina where I grew up and said I would never return."*

She returned.

Kinston it was, population twenty thousand—plus one ghost. Vivian and Ben opened the Chef & The Farmer in 2006 in what was once an old mule barn.

"There are a lot of challenges to opening a

restaurant," Vivian tells me, and Ben agrees. I have returned to town after all, sooner than expected, to interview them at the Chef & The Farmer, which, despite all the attention it has attracted, despite the glare and glamour, is cozy and comfortable.

They insist the odds were against them, especially since Kinston at the time was located in one of the poorest congressional districts in the nation. But they plowed ahead with the thought of taking traditional southern dishes and updating them—*"Thoughtful, creative cooking rooted in this region's ingredients and traditions,"* states the restaurant's web site.

Vivian drew on her memories of southern dishes and added artful touches. Ben did, too. He *is* an artist and went about decorating the restaurant with many of his colorful abstracts.

"The first day we opened we had eighty-eight guests," Ben says. "Which is a lot."

"Which is a real lot," adds Vivian. "And we have never been slow."

But they had been skeptical. And initially, so were their customers. "People used to come in, and they had this look on their faces, like, 'Is this really gonna be worth my time?'" Vivian says. "'I mean, I'm having dinner in Kinston, and I've driven two hours here. I can't believe this. This is going to be terrible.'"

And yet today, people visit the Chef & The Farmer from all over the world. Part of that has to do with the popularity of the TV show. Vivian hosted *A Chef's Life* for five seasons and won a Peabody Award. Her 2016 cookbook and memoir, *Deep Run Roots,* earned her other prestigious honors. "I believe in cooking food that has a story behind it and integrity to it," she's quoted as saying. "Food with a very specific sense of place."

And about that place.

Kinston has turned around in the years since my ghost story, dramatically so, and the Chef & The Farmer is largely responsible. It is so successful that Vivian and Ben have opened another restaurant in town. Somebody else opened a popular brewery, Mother Earth, and turned an old bank into a boutique hotel. Kinston has suddenly become a destination.

Which makes me think of the ghost.

I wonder if the pesky little thing has also changed. I bet it has. No more slamming doors and haunting voices.

These days, I'd like to think it's a happy ghost because of the spirited company it now enjoys in Kinston.

THE HEN & THE HOG

16 KING ST., HALIFAX, NC 27839, (252) 583-1017,
THEHENTHEHOG.COM

The food is delicious. And so is the history.

Halifax is known for the Halifax Resolves, adopted April 12, 1776, when North Carolina leaders met in the town by the river and laid their lives on the line.

All eighty-three men voted unanimously to cut ties from Britain. There had long been rumblings for independence, but none of the colonies had taken the first formal step, not until Halifax did on April 12. Weeks later, on July 4, the founding fathers adopted the Declaration of Independence, and perhaps the fathers found their resolve in the Halifax Resolves. Perhaps it gave them the confidence to bravely cast their lot for freedom.

History rightfully celebrates what happened in Philadelphia; the vote for independence far overshadows what happened in Halifax. The Declaration was the prize, the Resolves a mere historical footnote.

But North Carolina remembers. April 12, 1776, is proudly emblazoned on the state flag, and *First in Freedom* is stamped on many North Carolina license plates.

The Hen & The Hog remembers, too.

It's a restaurant on the main street in Halifax—there aren't many streets in Halifax; the town has a population of just over two hundred. And yet something is definitely happening inside The Hen & The Hog. It's nearly always packed—no telling how many orders of shrimp and grits the waitresses serve each day. Plus, pimento cheese fritters and chicken wraps, hamburgers and Shrimp Po Boys, wedge salads and chocolate cobblers.

"Awesome," says the baby-faced cook. He's biased, of course, but states his opinion anyway—as the founding fathers did, and good thing they did. "We have a good vibe," he says. "Good kitchen staff, good team. We have a good connection."

A connection to history. The restaurant *feels* historic, especially with its wooden floor that seems to stretch forever—and into the past. The room is spacious, the ceiling high, and three patriotic murals tower above. They are American flags painted on the second-story wall, each flag distinct, representing the United States through time: 1776, 1876, 1976. The open staircase that leads to them is equally eye catching. It has thirteen steps, one colony painted on each riser.

The woman who opened The Hen & The Hog took a bold step herself back in 2015. "You opened a restaurant in a town of two hundred?" I ask.

"People thought I had lost my mind," she says.

Patterson Wilson grew up in Halifax and later became an executive with Marriott International, traveling the world, designing hotels. Whenever she'd return home, it would pain her to see yet another shop out of business, more boards nailed over empty windows. *Somebody's gotta do something,* she thought, which might have been

what those eighty-three men mulled over in April 1776. Now it was Patterson's turn, and she resolved to save Halifax.

She bought a sad-sack building and started renovating. "The building was falling down," she says. "You could see the sky." People did think she had lost her mind.

But they don't anymore. The restaurant is bustling, just as the town was three centuries ago. Today, people come from across the state and beyond to dine on beef filets and salmon pasta. They also tend to learn more of the town's history and appreciate its revolutionary past.

"I am ecstatic," Patterson says, as she should be. Contractors have begun to follow her lead and renovate other local buildings, and I have a feeling the town of two hundred has a promising future, built largely on its patriotic past.

Patterson folds her arms. "People said, 'Nobody's coming to Halifax.' And just look around." It's lunchtime, and patrons are smiling and laughing; the tables are full, and so are the waitresses' hands. More shrimp and grits. And good wine and rich history.

"Best time of my life," Patterson says.

CLAUDINE'S RESTAURANT

500 S. MAIN ST., RICH SQUARE, NC 27869, (252) 539-2266

"I hear you're the fried-chicken lady."

"I am," she says. "Best chicken west of the Mason-Dixon Line." She flashes me a wide smile. "And great hamburger steak." She chops at chunks of meat simmering on the grill, then goes to scooping chicken salad out of a tin and piling it on a sandwich. She has to multi-task. The fried-chicken lady is the cook, the kitchen her castle. "Everything's good," she says.

"Oh, and on Sundays I love to come and get their ham and cabbage," says a lady in the eating area. "And the crumb pudding. You've heard about that."

"The what?"

"Crumb pudding." She rolls her eyes as if the mere thought of it has floated her to heaven, though her feet remain planted in Rich Square.

It's a quiet rural area in Northampton County, full of farmland and sleepy streets, and yet it's tough to grab a parking spot at Claudine's Restaurant, much less find an empty table.

"Most of the time there are no seats left," says a man hunkered over his lunch as if protecting it. He's ordered a plate full of pan trout, the day's special.

It's an older crowd enjoying a weekday lunch. I meet a longtime doctor whose practice is right next door—he says he's been known to eat three meals a day at Claudine's. I'm introduced to a cotton farmer named Jimmy known for his efforts at battling the boll weevil; his land is just down the road a spell. And there's a table full of hunters, dressed in fatigues, who don't utter a word; they're all gnawing at the fried-chicken lady's fried chicken.

I have to wait a while before corralling owner Kathy Whitley, possibly the busiest person in Rich Square, and when I do, she doesn't talk about herself, but about her mom, Claudine. "She worked in a knitting factory and had a big dream," Kathy says. That dream was to open her own restaurant, and in 1979 she took the chance, built the building with borrowed money, and over time proudly paid off the loan. "She worked very hard," Kathy says. "Seven days a week."

Claudine lived long enough to see her dream flourish. "Folks come from all over to eat here," Kathy says. "I have people from Raleigh, Virginia Beach."

"Virginia Beach?" I say. That's got to be about a two-hour drive. "Coming to Rich Square?"

Kathy nods, and her eyes drift past my shoulder. I look around to see her mom's picture on the wall. Claudine smiles.

"Oh, she was just a really nice person," says Jimmy, the cotton farmer, his thinning hair the color of his crop, which he saved from the irksome boll weevil. "I tried to get her to adopt me, but she wouldn't do it," he says with a grin. The wily farmer clearly has a sense of humor. "Best place in the world," he says, and this time I'm sure he's not pulling my leg. "It's kept *me* livin', I know that."

I admire Claudine's picture again and wonder if she's smiling down from heaven. Which makes me think of the crumb pudding, and yes, I think I'd like to try it.

Some of the fried-chicken lady's famous fried chicken, too.

WALTER'S GRILL

317 E. MAIN ST., MURFREESBORO, NC 27855, (252) 398-4006

I'm not there on Chicken Pie Day; otherwise, I'd order the chicken pie.

But I'm happy with my cheeseburger, topped with lettuce, tomato, extra mayo, and melted American cheese oozing down the sides. I let it cool a bit, and while waiting I trace the lines of graffiti zigzagging across my tabletop.

I'm sitting in one of the wooden booths and wonder about the crudely carved names beneath my fingers. I bet some belong to former students at Chowan College, now Chowan University, just up the street, kids hoping to leave their mark on the future. I wonder if they achieved success—or if they're even still alive. How long has it been since they left their mark at Walter's Grill?

I at last lift my burger, which leaves its mark on my fingers—juicy indeed—and I'm about to take a bite when Betsy walks up. Betsy Theodorakis and her husband, Bill, own Walter's Grill. The restaurant's original owner was a man named Walter who opened it on Main Street in Murfreesboro in 1943.

Betsy is friendly and bubbling with stories about the town. "While you're here, you should to do a piece on the famous Gatling Gun," she says. "You know, Gatling grew up in Murfreesboro. And Gatling's brother—did you know he built the first airplane in America, even before the Wright Brothers?" She assures me it's true and that he used his grandma's chair off her front porch as the pilot seat.

I put my unbitten burger back on my plate.

She tells me about the tiny ferry nearby that crosses the Meherrin River; it carries just two cars, and the trip takes thirty seconds. "Oh, and the museum up the street," she says and launches into a story about a world traveler who collected everything from mouse traps to bedpans, all displayed in the Jeffcoat Museum around the corner.

"Bedpans?" I ask. She nods.

The phone rings.

It's a rotary dial with a curly-cue cord on the wall by the grill, and it's been ringing constantly since I've entered. Waitresses usually snatch it, and I assume folks are calling in orders. But not always, Betsy says. "People call and say, 'Do you know that man who used to own the hardware store? What's his name? Have you got his phone number?' We get calls like that all the time." She laughs and tells me Walter's Grill has become the town's unofficial Chamber of Commerce. "It's this place, and our willingness to say, 'Hold on just a minute. I'll look up his number for you.'"

Somebody shouts to Betsy; this time, the phone's for her—maybe the man from the hardware store thanking her for steering him some business. Bill, meanwhile, is busy grilling burgers and hot dogs. He's got a full counter, though I'm sure he's used to it. He and Betsy have owned the restaurant for almost three decades, and together they've served generations of customers.

I wonder again at all the names at my table, people who sat where I sit. I bet they enjoyed a good meal at Walter's Grill, maybe lots of them.

The phone rings again—and again—but it's my cheeseburger that's calling me. I lift it to my mouth—juicy and cheesy—and take the biggest bite possible. Fantastic!

I know this won't be my last trip to Murfreesboro and Walter's Grill. I'll be back for the food and all the other stories and to visit again with the names at my table.

If I time it right, I'll return on Chicken Pie Day.

THE COUNTRY SQUIRE

STATE RD. 24 BUSINESS, WARSAW, NC 28398, (910) 296-1727

A seventy-two-ounce steak!

It's called the 72-Oz. Kilt Buster. The restaurant owner is originally from Scotland where kilts are rather fashionable. Iris Lennon speaks with a thick brogue and seems quite at home in an English setting.

The Country Squire has the feel of a British pub, the interior filled with dark wood and heavy beams. The light is low, candles flicker, and a full suit of armor stands guard in the lobby. It's like a medieval time warp in rural Duplin County.

If the place sounds a bit haunting, well, it is. But that's also its appeal, that and the 72-Oz. Kilt Buster, which I suppose can be both appealing and frightening. The menu offers an array of meat, including the house favorite Korean Barbecued Beef, plus fish, pasta, and sandwiches.

There's also the ghost.

"The dart board on the wall over there," Iris says. "One Saturday night, several guests were enjoying dinner when three darts come out the board and went across the room." She tells me the darts *flew* across the room, traveled six or seven feet, before scattering on the floor.

"We've had guests come up and say, 'Do you have ghosts here? I just had someone follow me into the ladies' room.' I mean, you hear doors opening and closing, chairs moving."

Iris explains much of this while showing me through the restaurant, which includes not just one dining room but several. I almost forget I'm in Duplin County, for the place has the feel of the Fox & Hound in the English Cotswolds.

In one room, legless tables hover above the floor, held in place by thick chains bolted to the ceiling; the chains offer another steely touch. "All the chains were doing this," Iris says and shakes one rather violently, rattling the links. "Shook on their own, no one around." The room itself seems to groan.

She details the history of the Country Squire. A man named Joe West built it in 1961, a schoolteacher who dreamed of owning his own restaurant, and though people said he was crazy to build in such a rural area, he did it anyway and lived long enough to enjoy it.

Iris explains that part of the restaurant dates to a much earlier era. She says an old house from down the road was moved and added to the restaurant. "A woman died in that house," she says, her Scottish brogue coating her words with an icy chill. Maybe she's just playing to the camera, but if so, she seems serious about the role.

She shows me a picture of the house the woman died in and taps the bottom corner. "Right here," she says. "A wee girl's head peeping out." I lean close, and yes, a child appears to be peeking from the lower window.

Iris tells me about another oddity, a photograph taken during a wedding celebration at the Country Squire. One of the guests was posing for the picture but then turned her head at the very moment it was snapped. "The reason the lady turned was because the wee girl was standing beside her." Iris shows me the picture. In the corner is a blurry image of what looks like a little girl.

I ask Iris if she really believes all this is true, and she nods quite vigorously. "Yes, I really believe." But she also admits it's fun having a ghost at the Country Squire. "Oh, definitely. I mean, think how boring life would be if darts weren't flying across the room."

The Country Squire is definitely not boring, not with the wee girl, the rattling chains, the suit of armor, and flickering candles.

Or the 72-Oz. Kilt Buster.

MELVINS'

133 W. BROAD ST., ELIZABETHTOWN, NC 28337, (910) 862-2763

Melvins' serves fast food. Food served fast.

The two girls at the counter are amazing, the way they call out orders to the grill cooks, wrap the orders, and ring them up, one girl talking, the other repeating, back and forth and back again.

"One, no onions."

"One, no onions."

"Hot dog all the way."

"Hot dog all the way."

"Cheeseburger, chili, ketchup."

"Cheeseburger, chili, ketchup."

"Two, no chili."

"Two, no chili."

I've strung wireless microphones on both counter girls, and the action is terrific, and fast, and so is the ping-ponging sound. Except I'll be forced to listen to all that sound later . . .

"Hot dog, onions, ketchup."

"Hot dog, onions, ketchup."

"Tea, no ice."

"Tea, no ice."

I'll have to write down everything they say and weave many of those countless snippets into my story.

"Two all the way, no slaw."

"Two all the way, no slaw."

"Double, no mustard, ketchup."

"Double, no mustard, ketchup."

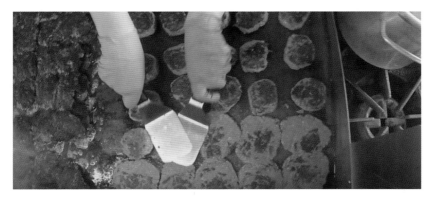

"We can put a hot dog on the counter every five seconds," owner Randy Harris says, and I can believe it having witnessed it. Place an order with one girl, and five seconds later the other girl has it wrapped and ready. Of course, the grill cooks are fast, too. "People will come in and ask for, like, forty hamburgers, and it won't take us but a few minutes to get that done, and it's all made to order."

Randy has owned Melvins' for just a few years. He took over from the longtime owners and knew he'd have his doubters; people don't like change. Randy is a thin man with a mustache and admits to a mechanical mind and keen business sense. His goal was to have the best meat and fastest service.

"Five seconds," he assures me. "It's very synchronized." And very successful; people soon shrugged off the management change and welcomed the speedy service. Randy pulls up a picture from his phone and shows me a Saturday crowd. The line forms a ring inside the restaurant, but the line moves fast, he says. "It's the pace that's different from everybody else."

Melvins' is clearly an Elizabethtown institution and has been since 1938. "I been coming here fifty years," says an older man lounging in a booth, his legs partly stretched on the vinyl cushion. "I believe every day is a hamburger day." I wonder how many burgers he's eaten over the years—and how long before he's down for a nap.

I meet a fella named Bob at a table. "I'm fifty-six," he says, "so I probably been coming here fifty-seven years in one form or another." He laughs and tells me he loves Bladen County, the friendly people and good food at Melvins'. "I'm a one-of-each, all-the-way kind of guy," he says, meaning both dogs and burgers, smothered.

"Cheeseburger, two hot dogs, heavy chili with ketchup."

"Cheeseburger, two hot dogs, heavy chili with ketchup."

"One all the way, hot sauce."

"One all the way, hot sauce."

It's excruciating listening to the sound pile up, knowing my work-load swells with every sentence, and yet I'm a sucker for punishment. I step to the counter and burden myself a bit more.

"I'll take two all the way with extra mustard, please, and a diet Coke."

"Two all the way, extra mustard. Diet Coke."

"Two all the way, extra mustard. Diet Coke."

It's in my hands in five seconds. And it doesn't take much longer to reach my belly.

WARD'S GRILL

706 S. MADISON ST., WHITEVILLE, NC 28472, (910) 642-2004

He arrives at the restaurant at three in the morning every morning and prepares for the crowd. The place opens at 7 a.m.

"Hot dogs and hamburgers for breakfast?"

"Yes, sir," Junior says. Junior is older than my dad.

"Daddy's been here over fifty years," says his daughter, Kandle.

They stand five feet from each other behind the counter, Junior at the grill, Kandle at the register. She greets each customer and calls out their order. "No onions, extra chili, Daddy." By the time she makes change, Junior has the hot dog in front of her on wax paper. Kandle wraps it, bags it, and then it's on to the next person in line. "Two more cheeseburgers, Daddy, no onion."

Junior doesn't say a word—well, he does say one when I throw him another question. "Fifty years, why have you kept at it so long?"

"Dedication."

He's a small man with his eyes fixed on the grill, feet fastened to a single spot. He doesn't move; only his hand does, the one with the spatula.

"Two burgers and one dog all the way, Daddy."

He's calm, collected, and quiet, even when the line is twenty deep like it is now; it stretches beyond the door. Ward's Grill is take-out only, no room for tables and chairs. And no time for Junior to talk much.

"Nowhere can you get a cheeseburger like this," a man in line says; he's about nineteen feet back, but no big deal. He shrugs and points toward Junior. "He gets the burgers out fast."

Ward's opened in 1947, and it's been in the same spot in downtown Whiteville ever since. "This is a slow day," Kandle says between wrapping hot dogs and grabbing drinks. I wonder just how deep the line can go; it's not even noon yet—burgers and dogs for breakfast. "No onions, extra chili, Daddy."

I catch a breather outside. It's nice visiting Columbus County, two hours south of Raleigh and minutes north of South Carolina. The day is sunny, the street lazy, and I stand at the curb watching Ward's blue awning yawn in the breeze. A man carrying a brown paper bag exits beneath it.

"I been coming here since I was a little boy," he says. He carries the bag with both hands. "Two cheeseburgers and two hot dogs. Two to get me home, and two when I get there." He laughs and heads on down the street.

I watch him go and find I envy him. I envy him because I bet he'll be back tomorrow.

Maybe at 7 a.m.

PAUL'S PLACE
FAMOUS HOTDOGS

11725 US-117, ROCKY POINT, NC 28457, (910) 675-2345

Window down, beach bound. Gotta stop at Paul's Place.

It's on the way to Wilmington but not on Interstate 40. Highway 117 parallels 40 and takes its time meandering south from Wilson, through Goldsboro and Mount Olive, past Warsaw and Burgaw, and at last dillydallys into Rocky Point. Thirty minutes to go before sand and sun. But first, a dog and a Coke.

It's a big wide building for a little town and a packed parking lot for such a lazy alternate route. The structure takes up the whole corner and is painted white with *Paul's Place* written on it in red.

"On your way to the beach?" I ask a man who's hopped from his pickup, though I already know the answer. He's got a whiskery chin, faded T-shirt, baggy shorts, and he flip flops toward me before answering.

"Yep, heading to the beach and had to stop at Paul's." He gives me a thumbs-up and turns for the door. *Flip flop, flip flop.*

I have a fondness for restaurants with red-checked tablecloths; they remind me of my grandmother's kitchen table. Paul's Place has no tablecloths, but the floor *is* red and white, and the checkerboard pattern warms my heart.

The man who greets me is a slow-moving fella in gray shirt and pants, not what you'd call a beachy look. So close to the coast, yet so far. "Paul?" I ask.

"David," he says.

"David?"

He cracks a smile and holds out a hand. "David Paul."

We sit in a booth, and he fills me in on the restaurant's history, which has a pattern of its own. "My grandfather came here in 1928 and rented a little country store. That's where he started." Grandfather Addie Paul also started a family, and later Addie's son, Beverly, opened a store of his own and one day fired up some hot dogs. "Somebody walked in and said, 'Gimme one of those hot

dogs. How much are they?' And Daddy said, 'Oh, throw a nickel in the cup.' And that's the way it started."

David eventually took over from his dad, from Beverly, and from humble beginnings the place evolved into a hot-dog landmark. David tells me about a man from London who stopped in just last week. "Said, 'I made my four-thousand-mile trip to Paul's Place to get my annual hot dog.'"

"Well, I hope he thought it was good."

"Apparently he does. He comes every year." David cracks a smile.

We rise from the booth, and I go about my other interviews, and people are happy to talk. Many are indeed on their way to the beach, T-shirts and flips flops all around.

"It's like out in the middle of nowhere, but it's known all over the place."

"Wherever you're going, it's worth the trip to come get a Paul's Place hot dog."

"Great tradition. They've got it down, and it's good."

"But *why* are the hot dogs so good?" I ask.

"The relish."

"Famous relish."

"Homemade."

"Hard to find that flavor."

David sets me up at a table with two dogs all the way, extra mustard, and topped with that special relish. I eat and begin to understand why the man from London makes the journey each year. The chap sure travels a long way from home.

My eyes drift to the red-checkered floor, and I feel I'm back at my grandmother's kitchen table again.

Home.

BRITT'S DONUTS

11 CAROLINA BEACH AVE. N, CAROLINA BEACH, NC 28428, (910) 707-0755, BRITTSDONUTSHOP.COM

It's legendary.

Other places might claim they are, but Britt's really is, and it's open little more than half the year.

It's not unusual to see Britt's bumper stickers on cars around Raleigh, more than two hours from the famous doughnut shop. Doughnuts or donuts? Britt's keeps it short and sweet. Donuts.

Britt's has been making glazed donuts since 1939. Glazed only; that's all it serves. Other shops may boast of their wide varieties, topped with sprinkles or chocolate, or chocolate *and* sprinkles, or plump full of jelly. But at Britt's there's only one, and people can't seem to eat enough.

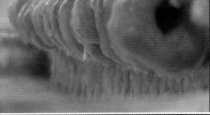

"Every time you get them, they're soft and light and airy," a woman with sunglasses and a tank top tells me. The place itself is light and airy.

Britt's is on the Carolina Beach boardwalk, and the exterior looks like a two-car garage with the doors up. Inside, ceil-

ing fans whir, and tourists in bathing suits and sandals stroll in, often bouncing toddlers in their arms. Or kids tug Mommy's and Daddy's arms, squealing in anticipation.

"A glazed donut, that's all we've ever made," says Bobby Nivens whose hair matches the color of his white donut shirt. Bobby began working at Britt's as a teenager and loved it so much he bought the place in 1974. He talks about a secret recipe and takes me behind the counter to show me the process.

I watch a man in an apron mix and knead the dough. But then Bobby points to rows of donuts dangling on dowels, and the best part comes when the apron man dunks the dowels into a vat of gooey glaze, then hangs them on racks to drip, drip, drip.

"Sugary sweet!" exclaims a young mom back at the counter, licking crystals from the corner of her mouth.

A man with flip-up sunglasses tells me he's been coming to Britt's for sixty years. "It's just simple. One kind of donut." He swears it's the best donut in America, and by the happy look on his and all the other faces, I believe he might be right. The place is indeed legendary, and the donuts are, too.

And that's not sugar coating it.

MOJO'S ON THE HARBOR

10 MARINA WYND, BALD HEAD ISLAND, NC 28461, (910) 457-7217, MOJOSONTHEHARBOR.COM

It's a sad story.

But it didn't start that way. It started out glorious.

"Literally bought a lot within twenty-four hours of stepping off the ferry," John Pitera tells me. "Went home, sold our house."

John is what southerners call a Yankee; he has the accent. His wife, Andrea, does, too. "And I had no intention of ever moving south," she says. "But I got off that ferry the first time, and I fell in love with this place."

Bald Head Island is remote and boasts of some of the state's best beaches. It's also full of dense woods. The island comprises twelve thousand-acres but has fewer than two hundred full-time residents.

I have the same feeling as John and Andrea when I step off the ferry from Southport and arrive at Bald Head. The village that greets me is gorgeous and peaceful, and I sit on the deck of Mojo's on the Harbor admiring the boats and watching the water wink in the afternoon sun.

"Fresh seafood," Andrea says. "Fabulous Italian food. Great cocktails." She's obviously proud of her restaurant, and I can see why. I think I could spend the rest of the day on the deck of Mojo's and the night, too. "This was their magic place."

She tells me about her grandchildren who used to visit every summer and how much they loved the island, exploring the woods, playing on the beach, and eating cheeseburgers at Mojo's.

"They started coming here when they were three years old," she says and shows me a picture. The photo is fantastic, a boy and girl, side by side on the sand, grinning at the camera. "Morgan," she says, pointing to the girl. "An amazing little force of nature. Bouncing, always bouncing. And John . . . Sweet and gentle and kind. And really smart."

I hear delight in Andrea's voice, joy bordering on laughter—but the laughter does not follow. "Your world just comes crashing to a halt," she says, and with that, *she* halts and cannot go on. And so her husband must try to finish for her.

"It was the fourth of July, 2007," John says. "A terribly rainy night, heavy downpour." He can barely continue; the rest comes out in pieces. "Connecticut . . . head-on collision . . . my daughter called." He shakes his head, and his eyes grow moist. "Thirty people from the island flew up to be with us," he says, and now Andrea does speak up.

"Anytime I felt like I just couldn't go on, somebody from the island was always there," she says. "Always there." She tells me Morgan was seven years old, John

nine. "At one point, we decided it didn't honor them in any way for us to live a life of sadness, that the only way to justify their deaths was to make our lives great." She turns her face from the water and tilts her head up at the building. "And so we gave them a restaurant."

I follow her gaze and realize she's not looking at the building so much as the sign at the top: MOJO'S. And then I realize, Mojo's is Morgan and John, their names combined. The sign is large and swirly, colorful, playful. "We bring joy to a lot of people in this restaurant," Andrea says.

We admire the sign for a long moment before turning again. The interview is almost over, the sad story at its end, so painful and yet the setting so peaceful. The sun glints, the boats rock. It is a glorious afternoon on Bald Head, and it is good to see Andrea's smile return.

"I had two amazing people in my life," she says. "And perhaps they will be again. I like to believe they will be."

SUNNY SIDE OYSTER BAR

1100 WASHINGTON ST., WILLIAMSTON, NC 27892, (252) 792-3416

I'm due to play hockey later, after my visit to Sunny Side Oyster Bar.

Beer league hockey, and you know how ice time can be. The puck drops at midnight. Who needs sleep?

But I don't think about sleep or hockey. Or about a peck and a pound, even though I'm at the oyster bar for a story. I'm wondering how exactly I'm going to mic the man shucking oysters so the cable won't show. It's a wireless microphone, but still . . .

Nate is a bear of a fella who grips a knife in one hand and a shell in the other. He has spent twenty-eight years prying oysters, though I doubt he's ever had a reporter slip his hand up his shirt while on the job. Yuck! And I don't just mean Nate's sweaty skin.

My mind flashes to when I ate my first oyster. I was a kid. "Here goes," I said, planting a smooch on the slimy sucker. "Sayonara!"

"You know they're alive," my friend said, two seconds too late. The one I downed was raw—and it didn't stay in my stomach long.

"It's a fight between you and the oyster." Nate says. He's the center of attention, the horse in the horseshoe; that's the shape of the bar, and onlookers occupy all thirty-two stools. They seem mesmerized, watching his meaty hands curl around each stubborn shell, forcing them open with a tiny blade, his tree-trunk arms gleaming in the overhead light.

He slides the shucked oysters into bowls, and people slurp them and sip beer and watch him go another round. "I don't know if I can last another twenty-eight years," Nate says, "but I'm gonna last as long as I can."

Thankfully for me, the oysters at the Oyster Bar are not raw. "Steam is coming up through here." says the steamer man. He's led me to a back room and stands by what looks like a freezer box. When he lifts the lid, a hot cloud billows out, and then he leans over and begins hauling buckets from the bottom, the buckets full of piping oysters. It looks like Nate's night has just begun.

Sunny Side Oyster Bar opened in Williamston in 1935. "It's known from coast to coast," says a man with watery lips, his oyster bowl nearly empty. Coast to coast sounds like a stretch—Williamston is a small town in quiet Martin County—but others say the same. One couple tells me they've been eating at Sunny Side for fifty years on months ending in R: September, October, November, December. Oyster season.

Sunny Side's owner saves me a stool at the horseshoe where I peer over the bar and see all the cedar shavings on the floor. Easier to clean the place that way, I guess, plus a little cushion beneath Nate's feet.

The big man pries open a shell and slips me an oyster. It's steamy but blubbery, and I stab my fork in it and try to block the childhood memory bubbling back into mind. I close my eyes and slurp, and down it goes.

When I open my eyes again, Nate is grinning and already prying another, and I slip that one down, too. And another...

I don't know how many oysters I eat but I barely make it in time for my midnight hockey game and then end up sweating as much as Nate, if not more. But not from skating hard. My exertion comes from keeping the oysters off the ice.

I play like a bloated fish.

BUNN'S BARBECUE

127 N. KING ST., WINDSOR, NC 27983, (252) 794-2274

A man named Bunn from Bunn opened Bunn's. But not in Bunn.

Bunn's Barbecue is in Windsor, in what was once a gas station. A couple of rusty pumps are out front, the tall metal kind with round tops and rotating dials. Except the dials don't rotate anymore. One of them is stuck on 99, as in 99 cents a gallon.

Mr. Bunn was from Bunn up in Franklin County but opened Bunn's in Bertie County in 1938. It's a humble little place with a splintery sign overhead that reads, WORLD'S BEST. The letters have faded, but regulars say the flavor hasn't.

"Been good for a good long time."

"Love it, love it."

"And it's not greasy. It's all meat," says a woman with gray hair, sparkly earrings, and a black blouse who's seated in one of the restaurant's white plastic chairs. "My mother always came to Windsor to shop, and we would always come here. It was a treat for us to come and eat barbecue at Bunn's."

Today, she's sharing a table with her husband, a small table; the place seats

only so many and yet is evidently full of memories. "Well, memory is part of it," says the husband who looks neatly dressed himself in a beige Polo. "And we just love the barbecue."

The couple also exclaims over the baked cornbread, which I see on their plates is especially thick with a golden crust. "Not everybody can bake cornbread like Bunn's," the woman insists.

I interview other folks enjoying lunch and often hear the term, *down home.* People tell me how grateful they are such a down-home place still exists. They're grateful it wasn't destroyed.

In 1999, Hurricane Floyd dumped almost eight feet of water inside Bunn's, a deluge. Locals thought they'd never see anything like it again; Floyd was supposed to be a five-hundred-year flood. But in 2010, tropical storm Nicole barreled in, and floodwaters swamped Bunn's a second time, rising more than halfway up the walls.

In both cases, people were shocked, saddened, devastated. They were also determined not to let Mother Nature rob them of an icon. They pitched in, bailed the place out and put Bunn's back in business. Folks are resilient in Windsor. And so is Bunn's.

It's just a humble little place with rusty gas pumps out front. And WORLD'S BEST written in faded letters on a splintery sign.

BILL'S HOT DOG STAND

109 GLADDEN ST., WASHINGTON, NC 27889, (252) 946-3343, BILLSHOTDOGSNC.COM

The screen door slams.

WHAP! The door smacks the frame and, *whap, whap,* bounces before settling. I wish I could get away from the door and the annoying whaps, but the place is barely bigger than my office cubicle.

"Yes, I'd like four all the way, please," a southern fella says to a woman behind the counter, one of three ladies standing together in a row. Lady 1 wields prongs, plucks red dogs from a bubbling vat and snuggles them into buns. Lady 2 smothers the dogs with chili, and Lady 3 wraps them in wax paper. The assembly line is quick and efficient; the women don't utter a word, and I can't say I blame them. Best to focus; the customers are almost out the door, though not quite. *WHAP! Whap, whap.*

Bill's Hot Dog Stand opened in 1928. Its history hangs on the wall—and has maybe hung there the whole time. The framed newspaper clipping is the color of an overripe banana, despite the protective glass. And yet . . . I peer at the picture included with the article and see—the *same ladies!* The ones in the photo are still at work, grayer but not slower, I bet. I turn from the picture to the counter and marvel at the whirlwind of arms, hands, mustard, onions, chili, the chili clumped with white beans.

"Oh, the chili is out of this world," says a genteel woman with beauty-parlor hair. I admire her blue-tint 'do and pearl earrings and am surprised to find her frequenting a place with no tables or chairs. But she exclaims over the hot dogs; they're out of this world, too, she says. "Love 'em, love 'em!"

Bill's is take-out only, though many folks slip outside to eat in the sun or shade and gaze at the shimmery Pamlico. It's a coastal town of ten thousand people, the first city in America named for George Washington.

"The *original* Washington," says the manager of Bill's. He's young, early thirties, but apparently knows his history. "Nothing's changed," he says. Indeed, many of Washington's stately homes still stand, some dating to Revolutionary times, and apparently Bill's hasn't changed from its early days, either.

"Everything's cooked the same way, prepared the same way," Lady 1 tells me when I chance interrupting the assembly line. But only one Q&A; the customer line keeps growing. *WHAP! Whap, whap.*

"If I had a nickel for every hot dog that's been sold here through the years, I wouldn't have to work anymore," laughs a man who orders three all the way.

"They're not good for your heart, but they're good for your soul," says another fellow with a lumpy bag in his hand. He laughs and turns and waddles into the afternoon sun, the screen door slamming behind him.

WHAP! Whap, whap.

YANA'S RESTAURANT

119 FRONT ST., SWANSBORO, NC 28584, (910) 326-5501, YANAMAMAS.COM

I once did a story about a great grandmother from Swansboro, a charming town in Onslow County, who had lived in the same house for ninety-four years.

The diner with the green awning on Main Street offers another example of consistency.

"When people come in, they say, 'Well, you haven't changed anything,'" says Evelyn Moore, otherwise known as Yana Mama. She's personable and welcoming. Swansboro, after all, is the "Friendly City by the Sea." Evelyn opened Yana's in 1983 and tells me about *her* great grandmother who was Native American and belonged to a tribe called the Yanas.

The tables are full, the jukebox rumbles; the lights blink to the rhythm of a 45-record. Elvis croons and peers from the walls, and Marilyn Monroe is in the house, too—they're even in the restrooms. A full-length cardboard cutout of the King greets women in the ladies' room; Marilyn is posted in the men's. The restrooms are popular.

"I just decided to do a fifties restaurant," Evelyn says, "because I love the music, and that was my time."

Now it's time to eat: breakfast, lunch, or both at the same time. "You might have something of everything at one table," says a tall waitress with a wide smile. "A burger with pancakes, eggs, a Reuben also. Everything homemade."

She mentions the fritters—actually everybody mentions them. Swansboro, the town, may be known for mullet fish, but Yana's, the restaurant, is famous for fruit fritters.

I interview a table of ladies plowing through mountains of whipped cream before finally poking into crust and scooping out spoons full of apples, bananas, and strawberries. "Amazing," one woman says, and they all shake their heads in agreement and reach for napkins. The fritters look like works of art, or at least they did before the digging started.

The cherry on top is the atmosphere of Yana's, the old-timey décor and friendly feel. Even the hamburger buns are friendly; the cooks use ketchup to squirt smiley faces.

One woman sums it up nicely. She's in a booth with a pancake so big it droops over the sides of her plate. "If you ever want to go back in time and figure out what that's like, come here. It's your classic diner."

Elvis croons from the jukebox: *Can't help falling in love . . .*

EL'S DRIVE-IN

3706 ARENDELL ST., MOREHEAD CITY, NC 28557, (252) 726-3002, ELSDRIVEIN.COM

Wedding receptions, birthday parties, class reunions. Ceremonies are sometimes held in the parking lot. Seagulls attend, too.

The parking lot is part of the whole experience; most people never step foot inside the brick building. It's a square block, smaller than my one-car garage, with a white sign across the top that lists the menu: Fried Chicken Plate, Shrimp Plate, Shrimp Burger, Oyster Burger, Steak Sandwich. Seagulls perch on the sign or dawdle around the blacktop; the seagulls are also part of the experience—and what a place to land.

It's a landmark. Come to Morehead City, and you've got to stop at El's Drive-In. "I'm telling you, it's good," a lady says from the passenger seat of a car. She's about my age with a squeal in her voice, and the more she talks the higher the squeal. "Where else can you go and just sit in your car and have somebody

come wait on you?" She waves her cheeseburger at me. "Go get you a cheeseburger, go ahead, get you one. Enjoy!"

Actually, I don't have to go get a cheeseburger; the cheeseburger will come to me. Park in front of El's, and almost immediately a lady exits the building, walks to your window, and scribbles your order. "It is Johnny-on-the-spot as far as service," says a man behind the wheel.

"Famous for shrimp burgers, super burgers, hot dogs," owner Mark Franks says. "Variety of things, everything good." He tells me about his dad, Elvin, or El for short. El opened the drive-in with his wife Helen in 1959. "Which was lucky for me," Mark says; indeed, for Mark's whole family. His wife, son, and daughter have all worked at the restaurant.

A man in a pickup leans out his window and tells me he's been coming to El's since 1966. "Since I was about four years old." I see he's enjoying a barbecue plate, and he tells me the slaw is homemade, an original El's recipe.

It's a pretty day, and there must be twenty cars in the lot, people with their windows down enjoying BLTs and fried chicken plates, poor boys and fish filets, and sipping on chocolate shakes for dessert.

"This makes me feel sixteen," the lady with the squeal says. "And not too much does that anymore." The squeal rises, and she waves the cheeseburger again. "Go get you one."

But it's the shrimp burger I want; that's what El's is most famous for. Friends back home with vacation houses in Carteret County have told me all about it: pieces of shrimp with tartar sauce piled between a bun.

My interviews done, I climb in the car and a lady comes to take my order. I tell her no hurry, and she walks back to the little building and disappears inside.

I don't mind waiting. There's a nice breeze, and if I close my eyes, I can practically see the beach. I can almost *hear* the beach. I definitely hear the seagulls, which don't seem to be squawking so much as singing. They must be happy. The seagulls are El's regulars, too.

Can't say I blame 'em.

SANITARY FISH MARKET AND RESTAURANT

501 EVANS ST., MOREHEAD CITY, NC 28557, (252) 247-3111, SANITARYFISHMARKET.COM

When a little fish market opened in Morehead City in 1938, the owners took pride in keeping the place clean and—sanitary.

It's the T-shirts that always stop me. I wonder how many thousands of Sanitary T-shirts are walking around North Carolina today; indeed, around the globe. I see them often in various colors: blue, green, yellow, orange, *Sanitary* scrolled in swirly white letters on the back. The shirts are as iconic as the restaurant, maybe more, and they make me think of the laid-back coast, the sun and salty air, and flounder and shrimp. But I wonder what others think: North Carolinians trotting across Europe, for example, *Sanitary* shouting from beneath their shoulders. Eee gads!

The fish market became a restaurant the same year it opened, rustic and simple with a potbelly stove and plenty of folks to feed. A large order of fish back then cost forty cents; today, the restaurant keeps a copy of the old menu on display.

"It's a wonderful story, because it's about history," says a customer named Ken, gray-haired and red faced; in fact, his face is crimson, I guess because he's so excited about the restaurant and its storied past. "You were at the Sanitary! Yeah, it was a big deal." Ken can hardly contain himself—he's a terrific interview. "In some ways, the Sanitary is the heart and soul of anyone who ever remembered the old days."

Shrimp, crab, clams, mussels, oysters . . . Inshore or offshore fish: fried, broiled, blackened, grilled. Steak, chicken, and pasta, too. So much to choose from—no wonder Ken's face is red with excitement. Though it could be from too much sun; the restaurant is perched on the Morehead City waterfront.

John Tunnell never tires of the seaside view. "I been working here, straight through, sixty-eight years." John is eighty-two the day I meet him and started work at age fifteen. "I used to be the youngest employee, and now I'm the oldest." He's a big man whose chest swells with pride.

Or maybe with longing. "Looks like you've got some beauty queens here," I say, pointing to a row of pictures on the wall. John is at the center of all of them, grinning in a sea of blondes.

"Oh, we've had lots of beauty queens," he says and grins again—his grin hasn't changed over the years.

I ask about familiar faces in other pictures. "Jesse Helms," he says. "Used to wait on him. And Chuck Yeager, man who broke the sound barrier. I met him several times."

He moves from picture to picture, recalling names. I've been told he has a photographic memory, and a framed headline boldly says so. "HE NEVER FORGETS A FACE," it reads. "THE MEMORY MAN."

The Sanitary seems to be all about memory: memories of the coast, fun times with family and friends, fresh seafood, and gorgeous sunsets.

In fact, the sun is setting now, and I take time to watch that big orange ball grow redder by the second. That's when I know, standing on the deck of the Sanitary, that this moment provides a memory, too—one of my own.

This memory belongs to me.

SAM & OMIE'S RESTAURANT

**7228 S. VIRGINIA DARE TRAIL, NAGS HEAD, NC 27959,
(252) 441-7366, SAMANDOMIES.NET**

"It's real beachy."

Beachy. The word fits. *Busy* does, too.

The waitress can stop only for a moment, and when I ask her what she thinks of the place, she has time for the one quick comment before dashing off into the beachy, busy, atmosphere that is Sam & Omie's.

I'm there on a summer morning, and it's all T-shirts and flip flops, link sausages and eggs, sunny side up. "A second waitress says she meets people from all over the world. A third one tells me she's worked at Sam and Omie's for forty years.

"Forty years?"

She laughs and assures me it's true. "Forty years, Honey," she says and rambles off, hefting a tray full of Belgian waffles, spinach-and-onion omelets, and Bloody Marys.

Oh, it's fantastic," raves a woman with a tan and a Jersey accent.

"Love it," croaks a whiskery man in a tattered hat. He's from Pennsylvania, on vacation on the Outer Banks, fishing and eating, he says. "Good home cookin'."

Oh, what a place, a jumble of tables too crowded for a tripod, but that's okay. Who cares if shouldering the camera is shaky? It's as if the whole room is moving anyway. How many waitresses? I don't know, but I see flashes of fire-engine red all around, the waitresses in their bright shirts, whisking trays full of scrambled eggs with bacon and pancakes pocked with chocolate chips.

"The fish cakes are phenomenal," cries a lady at the bar who says she swings in several times a week for breakfast, lunch, or dinner. Fish cakes make sense, and so does the crab Benedict I heard somebody order. Fishing is the hook; it and Sam are what started Sam & Omie's.

Sam Tillett was a Nags Head fisherman; Sambo is what he went by, and wouldn't it be good, he thought, if fishing folks had a place of their own, somewhere to grab a snack and coffee before rigging up and puttering out? He opened his little building in 1937. "And the guys would meet here and then they'd all go fishing," says Carole Sykes.

Today, Carole owns the restaurant and knows the history well. She also knew Omie, Sam's son, a fisherman himself and boat builder.

"The *original* boat builder," she says and tells me Omie built wooden boats by hand and willingly shared his know-how. "He started *all* the boat builders here. A very nice man."

A very Godly man, too. He used to bless the fleet each morning, delivering short sermons to captains and crew over a two-way radio. "He lived a great life," Carole says.

Omie lived to be ninety and died in 2019; his dad, Sam, passed many years before. Their pictures are on the walls, their names by the front door.

"The restaurant," I say, "what a legacy to Sam and Omie."

Carole agrees. "Oh, absolutely."

I wonder how many customers know the history of Sam and Omie's. Although they definitely know Sam and Omie's. "Eat here every morning on vacation," says a man from Raleigh who's with his wife and kids. He says they usually wait for a table but don't mind—vacation.

"People been coming here forever," says the woman working the register. "I mean, fifty, sixty years. They come back every year."

I can understand why. It's the atmosphere: beachy and busy with waitresses whirring as fast as the ceiling fans. "Everything good?" I hear one of them ask a table—and hear myself thinking, *Yes, everything's great.*

I've wrapped my interviews and added my name to the list. I'll order coffee while I wait and bet I won't drink half before a red shirt comes around with a refill. I feel like I'm on vacation myself, and I guess that's from being on the Outer Banks. But also from the atmosphere at Sam & Omie's.

Beachy.

CAPT'N FRANKS

3800 N. CROATAN HWY., KITTY HAWK, NC 27949, (252) 261-9923, CAPTNFRANKS.COM

The place is bright and happy and buzzes with energy. *Ziiippp!*

It's like being at your favorite laid-back spot at the beach on a Friday in early June with the whole summer in front of you. Life is good.

Neon hats hang from ceiling beams, and neon T-shirts are everywhere, too, and not just on the racks; half the people in the place are wearing one. "I've gotten a T-shirt every year for, like, the past fifteen years," a college kid tells me. School's out, and he's fled to Kitty Hawk with his girlfriend, a dark-haired beauty. They're in line to order, with *Capt'n Franks* printed on the backs of their shirts and franks just ahead. But it's a tough decision; the board is chock full: Texas Chili Dog, Boston Dog, Snap Dog, Corn Dog, Mac 'N Cheese Dog . . .

I've heard about the Chicago Dog. A lady at my church in Raleigh raved about it during coffee hour one Sunday. I thought she was going to grab me by the lapels when I mentioned my upcoming visit to Capt'n Franks. Her eyes sprang wide. "The Chicago Dog!" she cried. "You've got to get the Chicago Dog. The best!" She was so excited her hand trembled, the one holding her coffee cup. I prayed she wouldn't spill it and doubted it was decaf.

Corona seems the drink of choice when I arrive at Capt'n Franks. I interview a man from Ohio with a half-empty bottle, a lime slice floating in the beer, and a streaky sheet of wax paper where his lunch had

been. "I've had two of the Junkyard dogs," he says. "It's described as the works, and I promise you it is the works. Worth every cent and every bite."

He makes sure I see the black-and-white photo on the wall behind him. It's an aerial shot with a lonely building in the center and nothing else around save for sand. "What it looked like when it first opened," he says. "This was a stand-alone place, and it's endured all these years. That's really a spectacular picture."

I agree, it *is* spectacular and am surprised he's so keen on local history. But then, he's from Ohio, and long ago two fellas from Dayton also took a chance on the Outer Banks: The Wright Brothers.

I meet Harvey Hess, Jr., who owns Capt'n Franks and whose dad founded it. Harvey, Jr. is a man in his mid-sixties with a whiskery face; the whiskers are gray. He wears a T-shirt over his thin frame and asks people how they're doing and where they're from.

Harvey is the first person folks meet when they walk in the door; he's right there to take their order. "Regular or foot-long?" He jots on a pad, tears off the ticket, and passes it to a staff girl in front who clips it to an overhead wire using a clothespin. It's a makeshift zip-line is what it is, and I'm awed when she rears back and sends the ticket zipping down the wire to the cook at the other end who plucks it from the line and adds another dog to the grill.

"It's always been about the hot dog," Harvey says. "I mean, it's just always been about the dog."

I remember the Chicago Dog—the woman at church—and Harvey scribbles my order. While waiting, I look around and take in the

fun energy of the place: the vacationers, the Coronas, the neon hats. Then my eyes fall on that old aerial photo with the one lonely building. "There was nothing on this road for two miles in either direction," Harvey says when I ask about his dad and the chance he took and the foresight he possessed.

The door opens, more people enter, and I hear traffic rushing by on Croatan Highway, and I marvel at how Capt'n Franks started and what it's become.

"I'd have a revolution on my hands if I tried to change this place," Harvey says and tears off another ticket. The girl in front clips it with a clothespin and hurls it down the line.

Ziiippp!

WEST

Asheville
French Broad Chocolate
    Lounge, 209

Banner Elk
Sorrento's Italian Bistro, 203

Beech Mountain
Fred's Backside Deli, 205

Belmont
Byrum's Grocery & Grill, 186

Charlotte
Price's Chicken Coop, 180
South 21 Drive In, 182
The Open Kitchen, 184

Gastonia
Tony's Ice Cream, 188

Greensboro
Yum Yum Better Ice Cream, 166

Hayesville
The Copper Door, 211

High Point
Becky's & Mary's Restaurant, 168

Kernersville
Fitz on Main, 170

Lexington
Lexington Barbecue, 174
Cook's Barbecue, 176

Linville Falls
Famous Louise's Rock House
    Restaurant, 199

Marion
Jack Frost Dairy Bar, 197

Pisgah Forest
Dolly's Dairy Bar, 207

Reidsville
Short Sugar's, 172

Salisbury
Hap's Grill, 178

Shelby
Shelby Cafe, 190
Red Bridges Barbecue
    Lodge, 192

Valdese
Myra's, 195

West Jefferson
Black Jack's Pub & Grill, 201

YUM YUM
BETTER ICE CREAM

1219 SPRING GARDEN ST., GREENSBORO, NC 27403,
(336) 272-8284

Grandpa sold ice cream from a cart. He called one of his first flavors Yum Yum.

Grandpa's real name was W.B., and he started selling ice cream in 1906. In 1922 he switched from horse and wagon to brick and mortar.

"The original store," Clint Aydelette says and shows me a framed photo of an old building that looks like a castle on a downtown corner, big and brick with a rounded front. Grandpa did well.

And so did the University of North Carolina at Greensboro. Over the years, the college boomed and bought up land and eventually forced Yum Yum to move. But not without protest. Bumper stickers at the time read, SAVE YUM YUM, SELL UNCG.

They both not only survived but thrived. Yum Yum moved across the street, and today the newer building is also brick, though flat, with an awning out front and Grandpa's machinery in back, cranking away all these years later: bulky fans, metal pipes, steel vats. "All original," Clint shouts, competing with the clanking. "We're like the only small company in North Carolina that still makes its ice cream from scratch."

It's fascinating, the fact it still runs. I watch a girl settle a tall container under a steel spigot and pull the handle. Out slides rich layers of smooth, creamy ice cream that begin to fill the barrel. "What flavor?" I ask—I shout.

She straightens to meet me while there's time, a pretty twentysomething with sparkly eyes and brown hair tucked under a Yum Yum ball cap. "It's coffee, and it's really awesome," she says before fetching a second container.

"My niece," Clint says. "Fourth generation." I wonder if she's a student at UNCG, or maybe a recent grad, and bet her great grandpa would be proud.

We turn for the main room; Clint shuts the door to the back, sealing the clatter. The booths are full, and there's a line at the counter, and cones pass from clerks to customers, some with double and triple scoops. Hot dogs are also on the move.

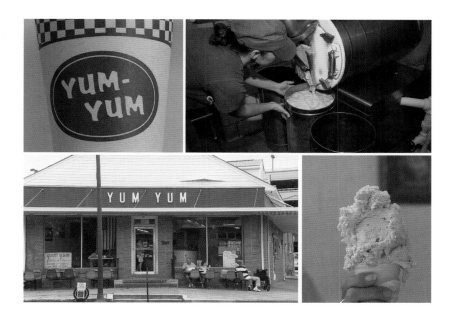

"Nowhere else can you get a hot dog like a Yum Yum hot dog," says a woman at a table with her daughter, a second grader probably, who happily swings her feet above the floor. The little girl nods when I ask her about the hot dogs and pipes up when I mention the ice cream.

"We both get chocolate," the girl says. "That way, my mom doesn't wanna eat all of mine and hers, too." Mom bursts out laughing. Smart kid—maybe a third or fourth grader.

It sure is a happy place, this simple place within cinderblock walls. A man tells me his milkshake is so thick he can't sip it, and it's funny watching him use the straw as a spoon and curl his tongue around the end. He's an older man but looks like a kid stealing a moment from his childhood.

I can't get the creamy coffee out of my mind—although I do wonder about Grandpa's Yum Yum flavor. Bet he had no idea his little cart of ice cream would one day evolve into such a beloved business. "Grandpa loved ice cream," Clint says.

And I'm sure Grandpa would be delighted to know how many people have loved *his* ice cream. Since 1906.

BECKY'S & MARY'S RESTAURANT

731 E. WASHINGTON DR., HIGH POINT, NC 27260, (336) 883-9917

There's no color barrier. No sign, either.

The restaurant has no permanent sign, just a white piece of paper in the window with *Becky's & Mary's* stenciled on it.

A man at a table tells me he passed fifty restaurants on his way to this one, never stopping until he reached the brick building in High Point near the corner of Washington and Hudson. "Good food."

And good feelings. I watch two women embrace in the middle of the restaurant, one who's white, the other black, and I figure it's been a while since they've seen each other—or maybe they saw each other last week or just the day before. In any case, it's a long hug and a great TV moment. They notice me watching and break their embrace but remain close, arms slung around each other's shoulder. The women address the camera, exclaiming over the wonderful food and camaraderie. "The friendships," one of them says, "that's what makes it . . ." she searches for the right word, "homey."

Becky's and Mary's Restaurant serves soul food. "Home cooked," Becky says.

"Word of mouth," says Mary.

Becky and Mary Ingram are sisters, Becky a few years older and chatty, Mary the taller, quieter one. "We look like twins," Becky declares.

"That's a matter of opinion," Mary says.

They opened the restaurant in 1973 and dedicated themselves to serving the best soul food around: fish, fried chicken, pork chops, pinto beans, corn, collards, candied yams . . .

A woman in line tells me she orders the stewed gizzards every time. "Oh, Lawd, if you never had stewed gizzards and rice . . ." Her eyes flash. "Oh, my gosh. Delicious!"

I approach a middle-aged couple at a table, the woman in a dress, napkin in her lap. "The food is excellent," she says. "Just whole food fixed really, really well."

"You never walk away hungry, that's for sure," says her companion. He admits it's been a few months since they stopped in—they're from the next town over—but that Becky and Mary both made a point of greeting them when they sat down. "Sweet people. Very, very sweet."

"They're faithful and friendly, and they give you more than your money's worth," says a woman sitting nearby." I hear *faithful* and notice another paper sign, this one tacked to the wall: KEEP GOD FIRST.

God and humanity. The restaurant embraces both. It's a large open room, filled with all kinds of people. "No color barrier," Becky declares, and Mary nods.

"You know, it works together real good," says the barber from across the street who's come in for lunch. He's also a preacher. "Treat others how you want to be treated. They call that the golden rule."

Golden rule, faithful, soul food, homey—words that help define Becky's & Mary's, a place many people find merely by word of mouth.

Other words help define the restaurant, too: *Stewed gizzards.*

FITZ ON MAIN

109 N. MAIN ST., KERNERSVILLE, NC 27284, (336) 992-1824

"You can't be claustrophobic and come in here, that's for sure."

The place is nine feet wide. "But we have regulars come for breakfast and lunch every day," adds the waitress, and I figure the regulars must either be over their claustrophobia or enjoy sitting elbow to elbow, often with strangers who wind up as friends.

"There's no Wi-Fi and no TV in here, and that's on purpose," David Fitzpatrick says. He's the owner, huddled over the grill. The burgers are sizzling, and I sense he's touched on something; I feel it as strongly as specks of hot oil on bare skin.

"Why no Wi-Fi and TV? What is it about this place?"

He leaves the burgers, backs away from the grill and folds his arms. "Just a sense of belonging," he says. "And . . . humanity."

David Fitzpatrick is the Fitz of Fitz on Main, established 2009. Although the place has been around much longer. Decades earlier, a fella named Charlie Snow paid $400 for an alley, put a roof over it and called it Snow's. The narrow diner on Main became a Kernersville icon. Some folks ate at Snow's every day, breakfast and lunch for forty years, until Charlie died, and the icon closed.

"It's about family and friends," Fitz says. He took a chance when he re-opened the restaurant and renamed it. People were used to Snow's and loved Charlie—whose picture, by the way, still adorns the wall. But Fitz picked up where Charlie left off—and he better pick up those burgers before they overcook. But another question while I've caught him reflecting.

"Did you realize that when you opened?" I ask, meaning the family and friends part, the humanity.

"Never ever realized that," he says and smiles and turns back to the grill.

He's good with the burgers and dogs, and, I imagine, with the omelets and pancakes when the doors open. But then, I guess he's used to a full plate. He's a retired high school principal.

"Lot of similarities between being a principal and a restauranteur," he says. "It's all about people. I mean, there are so many people that come in here who are by themselves, and now they hang out at Christmas, and they're part of our family."

It's a *close* family. Nine-feet wide. "Come on, guys. We'll squeeze you in," says the waitress, leading a group past the counter, along the skinny sliver, to the few tables in back.

"I been coming here since 1950," says a man on a stool midway down, and here comes his steamy plate of chicken and dumplings. Fitz doesn't have to reach far to serve the food.

"That's exactly right," Fitz says, and all three of us laugh. "And if I don't know them, I get to know them."

KISS ME, I'M IRISH, reads a green sign on the wall, and I think how lucky Kernersville is to have such a place. I bet Charlie Snow would be proud the old alley is still alive and well and bustling just like always.

"This is my retirement project," Fitz says and throws up his hands. No recess for the retired principal "Boy, what was I thinking?!" The whole counter breaks out laughing.

Fitz does, too.

SHORT SUGAR'S

1328 S. SCALES ST., REIDSVILLE, NC 27320, (336) 342-7487, SHORTSUGARS.COM

There once were three brothers who dreamed of opening their own restaurant.

The short brother, Eldridge, had a girlfriend, and one day his girlfriend said she wanted to dance with her short sugar. The nickname stuck: Short Sugar, which is the name of the restaurant in Reidsville, the brothers' hometown.

It's a cute story; people in Reidsville know it well, both the story *and* the restaurant. The restaurant is a staple, the story, perhaps, a stretch—legends can have a life of their own. But what isn't a stretch is the legend's end.

There really were three brothers. In 1949, Johnny, Clyde, and Eldridge Overby were excited about their new restaurant: Overby Brothers Drive-In, offering curb service and quality food. But two days before the grand opening, Eldridge was killed in a car accident. Johnny and Clyde were devastated but saw the plans through and named the restaurant in his memory.

Today, more than sixty years later, it's another busy afternoon at Short Sugar's. "Everybody who knows Reidsville knows where Short Sugar's is," says a man on a stool at the counter. He has a terrific view of the two barbecue pits a few feet in front of him loaded with hickory coals, glowing yellowy red, and racks full of hams and shoulders, all cooked right there. "Old-fashioned barbecue," the man says. "Kinda takes you back in time."

"It's just a way of life," current owner David Wilson tells me, a mild-mannered man with a thin face and gray mustache who enjoys both barbecue and history. He is respectful of the history of Short Sugar's. David kept the name, as his dad did when he bought the place from Johnny and Clyde. The restaurant passed from the Overby family to the Wilsons, and today it has touched three generations of Wilsons: David's dad, David, and David's son who also works at Short Sugar's. "And my son has a daughter who says she's going to be the owner one day," David says. "But that's a little early. She's thirteen," he says and laughs.

It's good to hear him laugh, good to see a lunchtime crowd; Short Sugar's draws a breakfast crowd, too.

"Food's fantastic," a lady tells me. "Great barbecue, great sauce."

Short Sugar's makes its own barbecue sauce. "We ship to Texas, California, Minnesota, Wisconsin . . ." David shakes his head, hardly believing all the places the sauce is sold. And all from a little place in Reidsville.

Where the dream never died.

LEXINGTON BARBECUE

100 SMOKEHOUSE LN., LEXINGTON, NC 27295, (336) 249-9814, LEXBBQ.COM

Lexington Barbecue.

The two words are synonymous, for Lexington *is* barbecue, long considered the barbecue capital of the world.

I feel as though I'm stepping onto hallowed ground when I climb from the car, that I've reached the barbecue apex and come to the meat of the matter. Not that my legs tremble, nothing that extreme, for the building is rather simple: long, white, and flat. But I do take a breath before walking in. I suppose my expectations are as bold as the parking lot sign: LEXINGTON BARBECUE, the towering letters emblazoned in black and red. My anxiety is magnified as well, for it occurs to me I've arrived at a barbecue kingdom the equivalent of Oz. And yet I fear being disillusioned, as Dorothy was in the movie.

The interior is also humble: tables and booths, a sizeable crowd and plenty of clatter and chatter. "The Honeymonk," says a man at the counter. "We always call it the Honeymonk."

Honeycutt and Monk were the names of the men who founded it in 1962, and people have combined the names and called it the Honeymonk ever since.

"Love it. Grew up on it as a kid," says a man with a loaded plate. "Moved away and come back every chance I get."

"Alaska, England, Australia." The waitress begins ticking off faraway locations. She's in her early twenties, Lexington born and raised, and yet she has served people from all over the world.

"A couple of hours ago there was a guy in here from Italy," says the pit master. I find my way to the back where it's serious business. The master opens the iron door to the oven, which is built deep inside a brick wall. Smoke billows, and he waves it away. "I can get up to thirty-five shoulders onto a pit. Shoulders is all we cook."

I look inside, as though peeking behind Oz's curtain, but in this case I sense there's real magic. There is certainly plenty of meat, shoulders lined shoulder to shoulder, plump, brown, and crispy. "Eight to ten hours to cook a run of meat," the pit master says. "Hickory and wood. We're known all over the United States." He shuts the iron door with a clang to keep in the heat. The curtain closes.

I catch up with the restaurant owner, Rick Monk, whose dad was the Monk of Honeymonk. "I have employees who've been here thirty-five years," he says and introduces me to the cashier whose son, daughter, and granddaughter have all worked at the restaurant. "It's history, part of history," Rick says between hellos with friends and customers. "It's rewarding. I love it all. It soaks you up, absorbs you, and it's part of who you are, who I am."

It's profound stuff, bold statements. "I mean, it goes on and on. It's an honor to feed them all." Rick has me convinced; the man means what he says.

No disillusionment whatsoever.

COOK'S BARBECUE

366 VALIANT DR., LEXINGTON, NC 27292, (336) 798-1928

The owners wanted a restaurant and log cabin. They got both.

Cook's is in Lexington but on the outskirts, at the end of a residential street, an odd place, perhaps, for a barbecue spot. It's a log cabin with thick smoke billowing from the chimney.

"Hickory coals, slab wood," says Jason Heitman who owns Cook's Barbecue with his wife. They've owned it just a couple of years when I arrive, but he tells me this is what he loves. I watch him throw another log on the fire, which sparks inside an iron oven. "Ancient as it gets," he says, wiping sweat from his brow and stoking the coals. "Back to the basics."

The restaurant boasts a long tradition. Cook's started in 1969 with a man named Cook who cooked outside. Cook cooked in his yard, and the 'cue he cooked was so popular he built himself a place out of logs and called it Cook's.

"Unique building with the wood," says a woman in a booth whose eyes travel the room. It's a warm, earthy room, and even the deer on the wall looks pleasantly at peace. No venison on the menu, but of course there's plenty of barbecue. I watch one of the cooks chop and another slather a rack of ribs with sauce.

"We have a big assortment of meats here," Jason says. Fish, too. He piles a plate with fried shrimp.

"Food is great, people are wonderful," a woman at a table tells me. "Very friendly. You're family when you're here."

The family *is* here. Jason takes a seat and stretches his legs. His wife Stacy joins him, bouncing their little boy on her lap. He's a toddler, not much older than a year, and wears a T-shirt that says *Baby Boss* across the front. He wears a big smile, too.

"Good home-cookin' food," Stacy says. She grew up less than a mile away and admits the restaurant is off the beaten path. She remembers eating at Cook's as a kid, though, and how much she loved it. And now she owns it.

She says this is what she's always wanted, a restaurant and log cabin. Stacy and Jason both say they're dedicated to continuing Cook's long tradition of serving great food, especially barbecue. They're dedicated to their little boy, too. I have a feeling Baby Boss is going to love growing up with Cook's.

The boy bounces, and his smile never quits.

HAP'S GRILL

116 N. MAIN ST., SALISBURY, NC 28144, (704) 633-5872

It's not always the food that makes the restaurant, although that is at least half the equation. The other half is the atmosphere. And at a place called Hap's, two halves make a roll.

The cook is rolling in rolls, stuffing them with dogs he's pitch-forked off the grill, one by one. And one by one, customers come; the line snakes from the counter all the way out the door and sometimes halfway down the street. But that's only half the story.

It's a skinny sliver of a place in downtown Salisbury, at 116½ North Main. It has half an address, which seems to sum it up. The place was once an alley.

"In 1927, they put a roof on it, made a building out of it," the cook says between equal parts spearing and grilling, half one, half the other, and he's nowhere near halfway done. It's not even half past noon.

"Oh, there's always a line," somebody in line tells me. A line but not much room. The place is eight and a half feet wide, and it's to-go orders only, no seating. Although the atmosphere's not half bad. A Little Rascals picture and Lone Ranger poster decorate the wall, the ranger's black mask hiding half his face.

"Hap's Grill has been here for years and years, and there's nothing like it," says a portly man in a red tie holding a hot dog slathered in mustard. By now I've slipped outside. The man stands at a tall table at the curb, the table bolted to a tree. "Well, you can eat more standing up," he jokes, though I gather you can spill more, too. His tie is half yellow by the time I turn away.

It's a pretty afternoon, and the curb is crowded with people standing and eating. Or sitting. One little girl couldn't care less; she sits half on the street and chomps. Too bad about the backside of her dress, but I'm sure it's worth it. No hiding *her* face, which is beaming.

"I mean, people take field trips from out of state to come and go to Hap's," a fella at another tall table tells me, nodding for emphasis, though I can't but help think he's telling me a tall tale. Field trips to Hap's? From out of state? But he keeps nodding, and no half nod, either. I believe he speaks the whole truth.

I learn from folks outside that Hap's is named for a man named Hap. But Hap's is also half of happy, and, clearly, the happy people who make a habit of Hap's delight in the dogs, appreciate the atmosphere, and yearn for yesteryear.

And at Hap's they feel they're halfway home again.

PRICE'S CHICKEN COOP

1614 CAMDEN RD., CHARLOTTE, NC 28203, (704) 333-9866, PRICESCHICKENCOOP.COM

A half dozen ladies stand behind a counter, lined from one end to the other.

"Hey, Sugar, how ya' today?"

"What can I getchya, Sweetie?"

"White meat or dark, hon?"

It's lunchtime, and the crew behind the ladies works quickly to fill the orders. The white-aproned staff in back moves here and there around stainless steel. It's hustle-bustle, chicken, chicken. The fryer man grips a long-handled wire basket and lifts it out of a bubbling swirl. Chicken, brown and crispy: legs, wings, breasts, thighs. He dumps the pieces into a pan, and they're quickly boxed or bagged.

"There you go, Shug," the counter ladies say to waiting customers. "You have a blessed day now."

My eyes light up at the activity inside Price's Chicken Coop: the busy staff, sweetie-this and honey-that, and all that fried chicken—fish, too—and the people clutching their bags and boxes close to their chests. "Oh, wonderful, wonderful," a woman says. "God gave them a vision for chicken."

Price's Chicken Coop skirts the edge of downtown Charlotte. Railroad tracks run directly across the street, and I watch the noon train whoosh by, not a chug, rumble, or squeal but a *Whooossshhh!* It's one of those sleek modern trains, like the trams at Disney World, a gleaming symbol of progressive Charlotte. I wonder what the comfy passengers think of the crusty brick building outside their window with all the people out front waiting to get in. I wonder if it gives them an unexpected jostle. A chicken coop with a crowd? *Whooossshhh.* Too bad for the train folks, for they've missed a magic kingdom all its own and not some Mickey-Mouse operation, either, but some of the best fried chicken in America.

Owner Steven Price tells me about the nationwide survey a few years back, "and we were in the top three." Steven is clad in white and bagging and boxing as fast as the other workers until I'm finally able to pull him aside. His tells me his dad used to run a poultry market but then tried cooking chickens. "And so he tinkered around with the

recipe and cooked a little bit and let people try it out, and it kinda took off from there."

It took off in 1962 and has been in the same location ever since. Same place, same chicken. "Honestly, we've been doing it the same way all these years," says one of the staff ladies. "It's wonderful, really tender and juicy."

The crowd swells, but it's all take-out, nobody waiting for a table because there aren't any, and so people are constantly coming and going. "They treat you like family, like they know you," says a woman with both a box and a bag. "And all walks of life."

And all walks of chicken. The menu board lists Chicken-White, Chicken-Dark, One Whole Chicken, Three-and-a-Quarter Pounds of Chicken. So much chicken, so many people. But the line moves fast.

"Here ya' are, Sweetie," says a counter lady to a customer and hands them a box. "You have a blessed day now."

SOUTH 21 DRIVE IN

3101 E. INDEPENDENCE BLVD., CHARLOTTE, NC 28205, (704) 377-4509, SOUTH21DRIVEIN.NET

Junior walks. For forty years he's walked.

"How many miles have you walked in forty years?"

He shakes his head. "I don't wanna know."

He carries trays while he walks, balancing them on his palm. Junior is the curb-service man at South 21 in Charlotte who brings food from the grill to people in their cars or to those gathered at picnic benches. He's pushing sixty, and he's thin—no wonder, what with all that walking. He wears a bright red shirt and smoky gray hat, similar to an old-timey bowler.

The place itself is old-timey; there aren't many drive-in restaurants around anymore. People pull in and park, zip down their windows and speak into a little squawk box. "A Super Boy, please, fries, and a diet Coke."

The woman inside—Maria—has her own squawk box, a much bigger one loaded with levers. She presses the lighted one. "Will that be all?" she asks. The voice on the other end says yes, and another lever immediately lights up, another customer.

Maria reminds me of a telephone operator in the days before rotary phones, when nasally voiced women announced, "I'll connect you now," and plugged cords into holes. I'm sure the women weren't all nasally, and Maria isn't either, but she is efficient, working one lever after another, listening and responding promptly.

Actually, she *is* an operator, the owner and operator of South 21, along with her husband. The box squawks again. "Two Super Boys, please, and a Jumbo Cheeseburger."

I'm not sure what a Super Boy is, but it sounds heavy, though I'm sure Junior can handle it. I understand he's as much of an icon as the restaurant.

South 21 opened in 1955 on South Boulevard, which was also called Highway 21. "They got the name from the road, and it just stuck," says the owners' daughter, Eleni, who informs me she just got married.

"Congratulations," I say. She also tells me she and her husband are Greek and spells both her maiden name and married one but loses me on the fifth vowel of the first.

Eleni pulls out a photo of her grandfather standing beside his two brothers and explains that they journeyed from Greece and together started the drive-in. At first, none of them could speak English, but they obviously attained success. Eleni is third generation. Maria is her mother, and her dad often runs the cash register. "So you work with your parents?"

"Ever since I was nine. Can't get away from them." She laughs, and I hope her husband shares her delight; I think he'll be seeing a lot of his in-laws.

I take a moment to marvel at the line cooks, four or five of them grilling and preparing plates, and not just burgers, but salads, plus "Famous Fried Chicken." The slogan is printed on the take-out boxes, while the marquee outside announces, "Special Fried Trout Today!"

I'm surprised by how many people at the picnic tables tell me they ordered fish, especially since they're sitting under the HOME OF THE SUPER BOY billboard. Although I do notice a fat burger on a bearded man's plate. "What *is* the Super Boy?" I ask him.

"A bunch of goodness," he says without bothering to list the ingredients; maybe the list is too long—maybe the toppings catch in his beard.

Several people tell me they've been eating at South 21 since they were kids and that Junior waited on them even then.

"Generation after generation," Junior says, balancing another tray on his palm. He holds his palm high, and the tray nearly rubs the rim of his bowler. I suspect it's a light load this time, which I'm glad to see for his sake. I bet the customer in the car ordered a simple salad. Or maybe he did order a Super Boy. Maybe two or three.

No problem. Junior can handle it.

THE OPEN KITCHEN

1318 W. MOREHEAD ST., CHARLOTTE, NC 28208, (704) 375-7449, WORLDFAMOUSOPENKITCHEN.COM

It opened in 1952, Charlotte's first Italian restaurant. WORLD FAMOUS, reads the sign over the door.

Inside are old photos and memorabilia, college pennants on the walls and pizza pie in the oven. The menu includes an array of Italian and Greek dishes. The same family still runs the restaurant, and the family's ancestry reaches back to Greece.

"My grandparents emigrated from Greece in 1907," says owner Christina Skiouris. Her grandfather began with a place called the Star Lunch in Charlotte. "All I know is it served fish sandwiches," Christina says with a laugh—Granddad kept it simple. "That was way before I was born." But her granddad influenced her dad, and it was her father and uncle who later opened the Open Kitchen. "They said, 'Okay, we'll do it.' And that's how they brought Italian food to Charlotte." Even though they were Greek.

Charlotte has grown over the years—and perhaps lost a bit of its identity—but the Open Kitchen has remained much the same. Loyal customers recall special occasions celebrated around checkered tablecloths.

"My boyfriend and I used to double date here," says a woman

in her seventies. She's alone at a table—a widow, she tells me—who thought she'd pop in for a nice lunch and some fond memories. "This is a throwback to a whole 'nother era."

The light is dim, the place cozy, and I can just imagine myself snuggled inside an authentic little place in old Italy or ancient Greece with a steaming plate of Veal Barcelona or bowl of spaghetti and glass of good red wine.

People tell me the line to get in used to wrap around the building. But of course, Charlotte is not like it was; it's fast paced, and there's more competition. And yet the Open Kitchen has not only remained open but stayed true to its roots.

The woman at the table is happy to talk. She tells me how good the food is, and for an hour or so seems happily lost in another world. I have a feeling she could stay here all day—and come back tomorrow, too.

BYRUM'S GROCERY & GRILL

4606 S. NEW HOPE RD., BELMONT, NC 28012, (704) 825-4106, BYRUMSGRILL.COM

NO WIFI. TALK TO EACH OTHER.

The sign is terrific, and I make sure Robert gets a shot of it. I'll definitely use the sign in my story.

Although my story's rocky start is *not* a good sign: lots of long, narrow-eyed looks at our camera. But of course, Robert and I are way out of our market. We've roamed west of Charlotte, to the town of Belmont in Gaston County, where people aren't used to seeing TV cameras; I doubt one has ever clambered inside Byrum's Grocery & Grill—until ours, that is.

"I love it. It's the best little secret for breakfast." An interview at last. Cindy sits at a table with her Bible and tells me this is where she does her daily devotion. And where she eats livermush with egg. "My day is off to a good start."

My story is, too, at last. It's the livermush that breaks the shell. People pipe up and tell me they often eat it without egg, just the plain grilled crunchy square, a southern specialty. They also tell me about Byrum's.

"Love to come here every chance I get."

"Friendliest people."

"Best coffee in the world."

Robert gets a shot of the coffee—and I wouldn't mind a shot of the coffee. It's breakfast time.

"Hey, y'all. How are ya'?" Libby greets folks at the cash register: Libby Byrum, eighty-three years old, white hair, white apron, colorful personality. "They don't know I talk politics, religion, and everything else," she whispers to a woman with a livermush to go, not realizing the wireless mic picks up everything she says—or sings. "You've—got—the—magic—touch." Libby sings in response to the lady who loves Byrum's coffee. "The—magic—touch."

Libby's whole family works at the restaurant. Her daughter Amy runs the grill. "We do a lot of livermush," Amy says, while turning hot dogs and hamburgers. "And we still do a heck of a lunch."

Amy's brother Greg prepares the plates. "Mama made something special to eat one day," he says, Mama being Libby. "Then that turned into a special every day." And that's how the grill was born.

Byrum's started solely as a convenience store in 1972, originally a red, two-story block of a building. Libby says her husband Olin felt the community needed a store. And then needed a nicer store. So in 1985 he had the building bulldozed and built a better one in its place and added a grill just so he could offer a few hot dogs and hamburgers. "Nine barstools, and that was it," Amy says.

But the grill soon outpaced the store. So Olin added on, and today it's full of tables and customers—and livermush and egg. Plus a toddler in a playpen behind the cash register. It's Libby's great grandson, busy with a rubbery toy, while his mom and dad and everybody else in his family run the grill.

"God has blessed us so immensely," Libby says, a bit teary-eyed now after sharing memories of Olin who has since passed away. "Oh, he loved this place. It's wonderful, just wonderful."

And so is my story. That initial awkwardness is long gone. I grin again at the catchy sign on the shelf: *No Wifi. Talk to each other.* Only now, I don't think I need the sign to help tell the story. I feel sure the camera has captured the friendliness and family atmosphere and people's devotion to Byrum's.

It has also captured the livermush and egg.

TONY'S ICE CREAM

604 E. FRANKLIN BLVD., GASTONIA, NC 28054, (704) 867-7085, TONYSICECREAM.COM

A man named Colleta sold ice cream out of a pushcart.

"My granddad," says Louis—Louis is a third generation Colleta.

"Was it the classic story where your granddad came from Italy with $15 in his pocket?"

"I don't think he had anything in his pocket," Louis says.

But the elder Colleta did have determination, and he had his name, and through the years the Colletas have carried on, more than one hundred years: Tony's Ice Cream, founded in 1915 in Gastonia, just west of Charlotte.

"This is what he did his whole life," Louis says, a proud grandson who flips through photos in a scrapbook he's propped on the counter. Louis is old enough to have his own grandson and seems to enjoy narrating this pictorial journey through time. "He went from pushcart to a horse-drawn wagon." We both marvel at the man and his horse; the pictures are fantastic. And people say the ice cream is, too.

"I love Tony's Ice Cream," says Judy, a grinning customer with a butter pecan cone. "I grew up on it, and I'm here just about every day for lunch."

Tony's has a full menu, and it's a sizeable place with booths and tables. "I probably been eating here forty-five years," a man tells me, enjoying a juicy burger and fries.

"This is a gathering place," Louis says. "That's what our history has always been." He can't seem to pull himself from the scrapbook, which I'm sure he's thumbed through countless times. The pages are dog-eared.

"This is back when we wore those old paper hats," he says and points to pictures of ice cream servers decked in white. "Man, I wish I had some of these cars." He taps a picture of a '41 Chevy with a bushy-headed kid squatting on the hood. "That's a picture of me," he says, laughing. "Later on, my dad took that car and cut it in half and made an ice cream truck out of it."

Louis is clearly enjoying this, relishing so many happy memories. Likewise, Tony's Ice Cream has provided memories for so many people over so many years. And it all began with a man and a pushcart.

"The history," Louis whispers more to himself than me. "We know the family business will continue," he says and flips to another page.

SHELBY CAFE

220 S. LAFAYETTE ST., SHELBY, NC 28150, (704) 487-8461

One day, Robert and I shot a story in Shelby and afterward grabbed a bite at the Shelby Cafe. Breakfast anytime, good coffee, and old photos laminated to the tabletops.

I ate and sipped and smiled at grainy faces grinning back at me. I read ancient newspaper ads by my plate and around my coffee cup. Elvis was in the house that night and on my table, and so were the Beatles from The Ed Sullivan Show in 1964. "Where Were You?" shouted the headline. Probably in bed, I thought. I was only two.

I looked at pictures of cars from before I was born, baby pictures, and photos of little kids. No use shouting, "Where are you?" The yellowy sepia tone told me they'd lived and died long ago. Yet here they were, memorialized in a certain sense, on the tables at the Shelby Cafe.

I never even bothered to look at my cell phone. I sipped my coffee, ate my eggs, and perused the tabletop, and Robert did the same. When we were done, we looked up at the same time and said the same thing: "We should do a story on this place."

"Eggs and livermush," George says. He's Greek, and so is his accent. "We sell a lot of livermush." I gather they do. The staff's T-shirts read, "*I Got Mushed at the Shelby Cafe.*"

The cafe opened in 1922, and it was Greek-owned even then. "They always fixed my chicken livers just like I liked them," says a white-haired woman named Dorothy. She sits at a round table with her grown grandchildren, and also at the table are the cafe's three original owners; their picture is *on* the table, beneath the clear coating. "They were my buddies," she says, grinning at the three men smiling up at her. "Every time I come in now, I try to sit at a different place where I can look at all the people and maybe recognize them."

The cafe evokes nostalgia with its wooden booths, all those old pictures on the tables and walls, plus the black-and-white checkerboard floor. And does anyone else these days make a triple decker club with the bread toasted? Even the sandwich feels nostalgic, especially with the decorative toothpicks that hold each triangular section together. I love the triangles and toothpicks.

"This is the cheese-burger club, and it's sooo good," says a waitress who has stopped long enough to point out everything on her tray. "This is the steak and gravy with fried okra and french fries, and this is our grilled chicken strip." I can tell I'll have a tough time deciding when we stop shooting and start ordering.

Robert and I work our way to the grill, camera rolling. "Two side cakes, one big cake, four scrambled, two whole wheat." The man in charge calls out orders, and by "cakes," he means pancakes, and they're huge and topped with dollops of butter. When the orders are ready, he slides the plates onto a shelf at the waitress pick-up window. All that food, and such a variety.

Regulars I interview use the words *icon* and *home* and *home cookin'* when describing the Shelby Cafe. George uses the word *blessed*. "We're very blessed," he says, and though his accent is thick, his gratitude is clear.

What's not clear is what I'm going to eat. But that's okay. No rush. I sip my coffee.

And read the table.

RED BRIDGES BARBECUE LODGE

2000 E. DIXON BLVD., SHELBY, NC 28150, (704) 482-8567, BRIDGESBBQ.COM

I was autographing books when a man walked up and flipped through the one I wrote about old-timey North Carolina restaurants, *Tar Heel Traveler Eats*. "Hmm," he murmured. "Red Bridges in here?"

"Red what?"

"Best barbecue in the state." He finished flipping, frowned, and set the book back on the table. "I know my barbecue," he said and turned away without opening his wallet.

Yet he's the one who opened my mind, although at first I was thinking a red-colored bridge or covered bridge or rickety historic bridge. Only when I started googling—red bridge, red bridges—did I discover the connection to barbecue and realize I'd found another restaurant story.

I wanted to get to that story because I was curious. He'd said, "Best barbecue in the state." Granted, the man was just a passerby, but he'd also said, "I know my barbecue" and said it rather emphatically. His frown was emphatic, too.

So I planned a trip west to Cleveland County and a visit to Red Bridges Barbecue Lodge in Shelby. And I suspected I might have to talk to my publisher about updating *Tar Heel Traveler Eats*.

※

The sign is classic Americana. It's a brick tower that leans toward the road with big swirly script on a backdrop that's both pale green and dark green. It reminds me of a motel sign or one for a drive-in theatre. The story is promising already—but quickly dims. In a good way.

I love the dark wood inside, the paneling and wooden tables and booths, and the bar near the entrance, crafted from rich heavy wood. The atmosphere is . . . "Terrific, terrific!" says a woman seated on a stool who's terrifically enthused. "Legendary."

The white-haired man behind the bar is hustling about, taking orders and fetching iced teas, but seems to have everything under control. The back of his T-shirt reads, "KEEP CALM AND PIG OUT."

The barbecue lodge is one long room lined from one end to the other with tables and booths. A genuine sense of enthusiasm also stretches the length of the place.

"It's the food!"

"You can depend on it."

"Oh, gosh, probably the best anywhere."

"Y'all need anything else, or are y'all okay?" The waitress is the very definition of southern hospitality, her voice sweet and syrupy, and I'm sure her pleasant manner is genuine, too. Her name is Natalie; she's tall with black hair and bright red lipstick. She's also the founder's granddaughter.

"My grandfather came back from the war, 1946, and everybody told him he was crazy, that it would never work, nobody would ever buy barbecue in Cleveland County." She suddenly stops mid-story to see to another table. "Y'all ready to eat?" And so her mom picks up where she left off.

"His actual name was Elmer Leroy," Debbie says and tells me everybody called him Red: Red Bridges, Debbie's dad, Natalie's granddad. "Elmer Leroy—I think I would have wanted a name change, too," Debbie says and laughs.

"He wanted to open a restaurant," says Chase, and now it's his turn to take up the story. Chase is Debbie's son and Natalie's brother, and he tells me about his grandmother, Lytle. "My grandmother was working in the mills," and she knew there had to be a better way, he says. So Lytle and Red opened Red Bridges. "And it was always successful and always paid the bills."

Chase is in charge of the wood the restaurant uses to cook the barbecue. "Hickory and oak, a truckload every night."

"Yep, cook with wood," says Natalie, who's back and full of energy. "Somebody's here all night long. Shoulders only. And if you come in and ask for brown, we know you know barbecue." She means the brown, burnt ends of the shoulders, often considered a barbecue delicacy.

I watch the cook in the kitchen cut and chop and the man next to him crank the handle on the hush puppy machine. "Hush puppy mix made from scratch," he grunts between turns. "Every ingredient, scratch."

Natalie and her mom and brother talk fondly of their customers and of Red, and especially of Lytle. "She was the backbone of the business," Debbie says, and Natalie jumps in.

"Oh, my gosh, I've never seen somebody work like she worked."

"I'm proud to be here. I love it," adds Chase.

I can't keep them long; all the tables are full. People come and go and come again. The big white-haired fella at the bar jots orders, rings the register, and fetches iced teas, and I learn he's been doing it for decades. The man is jolly faced; he's enthused. And he's calm. KEEP CALM AND PIG OUT. RED BRIDGES BARBECUE LODGE. I admire the sign outside, the swirly script atop the brick tower that leans toward the road as if waving people in. Americana.

I can practically hear Natalie now: Hey, y'all! C'mon and join us. What can I get y'all to eat?

MYRA'S

212 MAIN ST. W, VALDESE, NC 28690, (828) 879-8049

We drove by Myra's on the way to another story. "Look at that," I said, and we turned around and passed it again. Then we hooked another U and drove by a third time. We were late to our next story. But I also knew I'd found another story and added Myra's to my list.

I was eager to turn around again and come back.

Valdese is a pleasant town though a tiny one, a dot in Burke County, but it does have an eye-catching diner, one that screams 1950s, with hot-rod cars, swingy tunes, burgers and shakes, and fried bologna sandwiches—and maybe a little romance with your steady.

"Well, it's got the nostalgia to it," says an older man relaxing in a booth who would have been a fixture at a place like this a half-century before. "I like things to stay like they are, and that's why this restaurant has always been good to me."

I meet owners Larry and Audrey Earp and find we share something in common: U-turns. They were puttering through Valdese one day back in '77 when they spotted a run-down Tastee Freeze. "Two walk-up windows, very little business," Audrey says. But it caught the couple's eye. They U-turned for a second look.

"We said that would be a nice thing for us to do," Larry says.

They made an offer and bought the place, then added on and made it into Myra's, named for Larry's Aunt Myra who worked fifty-four years at a Valdese bakery back when the town was full of hosiery

mills. In the beginning, Larry and Audrey catered to the mills, and though many of them wound up closing, their catering business still goes gangbusters.

And so does Myra's, especially when classic cars from four and five counties around show up for the weekly, year-round Friday night cruise-in. "Good ol' American iron," says another old-timer who tells me he's a regular on Friday nights—and a regular for lunch, too. He loves the chicken salad and homemade chips.

The cruise-in might be another story, I think, and how about that? Valdese with *two* stories: the classic diner and classic cars.

I bet the hot rods don't hook U-turns. I'm sure they know exactly where they're going.

JACK FROST DAIRY BAR

2449 SUGAR HILL RD., MARION, NC 28752, (828) 652-1178, JACKFROSTDAIRYBAR.COM

It's closed on Sunday.

"Sunday was our most profitable day," Jim Burgin says, or rather, grunts. He's bent over, hands plunged into a tall bucket, mixing ice cream with a long spoon, and the mixture is as stubborn to stir as taffy. "We mix together by hand, and that's the thing that makes us unique," he says, panting. I lean in for a look and see a heavy sprinkling of pecans, which will become Butter Pecan ice cream.

"Isn't that cumbersome?"

"Oh, it is," he says. "Labor intensive." But also flavor intensive. It makes a difference, he says. "We're one of the last places to do this. I don't know of another."

I'm not sure I know of another ice cream shop closed on Sunday. Sundays seem like ice cream days if there ever was one. "In terms of spiritual things, it was one of the best decisions we ever made," Jim says.

His leap of faith—changing the schedule, closing Sundays—actually *improved* business, he says, or rather, grunts. "Thirty-six flavors we make by hand."

Since 1954, Jack Frost Dairy Bar has been making homemade ice cream, starting with Jim's grandfather who called his shop Burgin's Dari-Creme. When Jim took over, he changed the name to Jack Frost after a poem his mother had written. He's both a sentimental and dedicated man.

"This has been my life," he says. "How can I make this ice cream just a little bit better? That's my goal." He's also a man with both goals and faith.

"He's here faithfully every morning at quarter till seven," a man at the walk-up window tells me. "Anytime you come here and the light's on, he's in there."

The town, on the other hand, seems rather sleepy. I've always enjoyed my visits to Marion, a quiet place to stay when shooting stories in Asheville. Better rates, too.

At Jack Frost, people sit at picnic tables and savor creative flavors: Mango, Pistachio, Nutty Coconut, Butterscotch Ripple, Bubble Gum—that last one meant more for licking than chewing.

There's also Chocolate Peanut Butter Swirl, and I think, poor Jim; stirring the peanut butter must be exhausting. I wonder how he does it, the work he puts in and hours he devotes, but I'm glad for the recognition he's received.

VOTED BEST IN MCDOWELL COUNTY, reads a sign by the window. "Proud to have it here in town," a man tells me and tips his cone in salute. "Homemade and delicious."

And faithfully closed every Sunday.

FAMOUS LOUISE'S ROCK HOUSE RESTAURANT

23175 LINVILLE FALLS HWY., LINVILLE FALLS, NC 28647,
(828) 765-2702

The restaurant straddles three counties; all three meet under one roof: Burke, McDowell, and Avery.

"You're coming in through Burke," says owner Shirley Yager and points to the door. "If you go to the restroom, that's in McDowell. When you flush, it'll go through Burke and over into the landfill in Avery."

Shirley is a curly redhead, full of personality. The restaurant is named for her mom, Louise, who ran it for years until retiring.

"Here's a little history of the restaurant," Shirley says and shows me a scattering of black-and-white pictures tacked to the wall. I'm not impressed by the first one she taps; the only thing in the frame is a scraggly tree. But Shirley says that's how it all began, with that tree and a few local moonshiners who used to gather around it to drink. "Well, they got tired of getting rained on," she says and taps a second photo of a lopsided shack and explains that in 1936 the moonshiners built themselves a building. "And when the revenuers would come from whichever county, they would just move to the other side of the building. Home free," she exclaims. "They'd just walk over to the other county, and they'd be good to go."

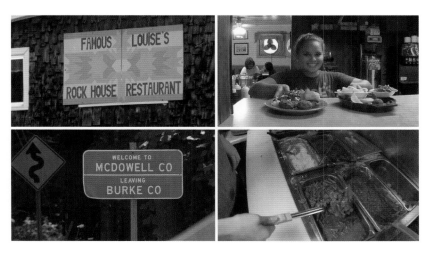

Famous Louise's Rock House Restaurant is not lopsided at all. It's built mainly of stone and sits at the intersection of Highways 183 and 221 in Linville Falls. Two highways, three counties—it's only my sense of direction that tends toward the lopsided, although the county signs inside the restaurant, dangling from each corner of the ceiling, help point me to where I am.

The atmosphere is country, lots of homey wood, and so is the food. Good country cookin': fish and fried chicken, green beans and mashed potatoes, burgers and sandwiches, and homemade pie.

Most of the kitchen is in Avery County—the sign tells me so—and I kid one of the waitresses. "You must walk through all three counties all day long."

She nods. "To get them their food and serve them their food." She's a college-age brunette, traveling on her summer break without leaving the area.

I notice colorful jars lined along the windowsills. Homemade jam, including Strawberry Rhubarb, a good one to bring home to my wife.

I also admire the mustache on a man bent over his hamburger steak, the steak smothered in gravy, the mustache an extravagant curly cue. I ask him which county he's sitting in, and he glances at the sign above. "Burke," he says with a grin.

"Your mustache might be in *two* counties," I say—I can't resist.

He laughs. "From where I'm sitting, you're exactly right."

I at last grab a seat of my own, one in McDowell County, and after enjoying my delicious Reuben, I visit the restroom in Burke County to wash up, then stroll to the cash register in Avery County to pay my bill and thank the friendly clerk. I've enjoyed my trip to Famous Louise's Rock House, nestled in the beautiful North Carolina mountains.

Now, if only I can find my way home. . . .

BLACK JACK'S PUB & GRILL

**18 N. JEFFERSON AVE., WEST JEFFERSON, NC 28694,
(336) 246-3295, BLACKJACKSPUBANDGRILL.COM**

It's a story told in past tense. Virginia's story.

"I was born in Romania," she said and described for me the danger of that war-torn country and her harrowing childhood.

In her mid-thirties, she at last attempted a daring escape. It was 1989, and she made her way to the river, fleeing in an inner tube without knowing how to swim. "Soldiers were all around, and if they heard a noise, they would shoot first and ask questions after."

I was riveted by the drama while perched on a stool at a tall table at her restaurant in West Jefferson. We sat in the middle of the restaurant, surrounded by a whir of activity: customers coming and going and waitresses weaving between tables. It was almost surreal, listening to her past life while people sipped beer and Bloody Marys and enjoyed enormous cheeseburgers and fries slathered in ketchup. Virginia's courageous ordeal was in the middle of it all.

Indeed it was, her story at every table, in the center of each table, a laminated page propped on a stand by the salt and pepper shakers, displayed like a menu but which read like a novel. "I had 1 percent chance to survive," she told me in her clipped accent, eyes wide, face animated.

In time, she found her way to America. "With $10 in my pocket." And only a single word of English: *Okay.* "I learn it from the movies. Okay."

She also learned how to cook. She wound up in the North Carolina mountains, and in 2008 opened Black Jack's Pub & Grill. "And that was my dream," she told me, her own restaurant. "My dream."

I paid close attention to everything she said. For one thing, it was loud inside; people around us were having a good time. The Bloody Marys seemed apropos, the kind of place you'd while away a lazy Sunday, or any day, for that matter: low light, good friends, juicy burgers, on-the-spot waitresses. "Refill?"

After a while, Virginia excused herself. She had to get back to the grill and invited me to follow. At one point, I watched her cook two dozen burgers at the same time. But she worked quickly, took orders in and got them out, and I had to hand it to her, everything looked and smelled delicious. She said she made the burgers using her own recipe. *"Best Burgers in Town"* is what the restaurant advertised, but people I'd met earlier told me they were the best burgers ever.

Virginia kept talking while she cooked. She laughed a lot and even found time to give hugs to some of her helpers. There was lots of hugging. And more to her story.

I should have guessed from her unusually close-cropped hair. Virginia had been diagnosed with ovarian cancer, and just like her escape from Romania, the odds for survival were not good. "Do I look like I have cancer?" she said with her hands in the air, a smile on her face, and more burgers on the grill. Actually, she looked like she was having a ball.

I tried one of her famous burgers and while I ate, re-read the laminated page at my table. It was a powerful story. And so was the line she'd repeated several times during my visit that day, a quote that seemed to provide the moral to her story: "Dream big, and don't let anybody steal your dreams."

POSTSCRIPT

In 2016, two years after my feature on Black Jack's aired, Virginia died of cancer. But her restaurant remains open—her son has taken it over—and so her story is not past tense after all.

I see her now in my mind: cooking, laughing, and hugging, lots of hugging.

The story of her life continues to inspire.

SORRENTO'S ITALIAN BISTRO

140 AZALEA CIRCLE, SE, BANNER ELK, NC 28604, (828) 898-5214, BANNERELKVILLAGE.COM/SORRENTOS-ITALIAN-BISTRO

My focus should be on my plate; the Veal Francese is tender and succulent.

But I can't take my eyes off the walls; the painting of artist Andy Warhol is a gigantic swirl of reds and yellows. Warhol's trademark eyeglasses are enormous, too.

I'm on a ski trip in the North Carolina mountains, enjoying a delicious dinner at day's end. I've crept down Beech Mountain to Banner Elk, to Sorrento's Italian Bistro.

"Everything here is just perfectly made," Angelo insists—Angelo Accetturo; his family came from Sicilly.

"But why Banner Elk?" I ask. It's a small village, out of the way, bordering on remote.

"My dad was coming up here on vacation, and he drove around town and said, 'This place really needs an Italian restaurant.'" Angelo's determined dad said, *I'm going to do it my way.*

Frank Sinatra stares at me, another mural-sized painting rich in detail, but the detail appears curiously patchwork. It's not art as smooth brushstrokes, but rather Frank's image seems formed from a collage, which makes the piece particularly interesting. Sinatra's blue eyes hold my gaze. Neither of us blink.

"The best ingredients," Angelo says, and I look away to savor another bite of my veal. Other entrees include, Vodka Pasta, Spinach Lasagna, Broccoli & Cavatelli, and the restaurant's number-one, the Tortellini Sorrento. "We're known for our food. And for the beautiful art on these walls."

He points at Andy Warhol, and I hope he's not nudging me to make an offer; most of the paintings are for sale. At least a dozen works adorn the walls, and judging by their quality and size, I figure the prices might be as steep as the black diamond slope I skied earlier.

Angelo surprises me when he says the Andy Warhol is his, that he painted it himself; he says he took up painting just five years ago. I'm in awe of his talent and take turns gaping from Angelo to Andy.

I also admire the works of *Paulette*, a name I see on several paintings, and soon learn the artist is Kent Paulette and that his studio is right next door.

"I experiment with each one," Kent says while at work on another piece. He scrapes the canvas in front of him with what looks like a small spatula. *Scrape!* Then he forms zig-zaggy lines with quick aggressive strokes. I wonder how he can be so cavalier with his work—but it works. I witness his latest creation come together; patterns emerge from the colorful abstract. A large fish jumps from the center—*Scrape!*—with a hook in its mouth. "I start with getting inspired by nature and music," Kent says.

He turns to show me his portrait of Taylor Swift on the wall. "I kinda went real wild with the shapes and weird colors." It's a face full of circles and squares and reds and oranges, and I must say, the pop star looks radiant.

Kent shows me other work—bears, deer, horses—both in his studio and around the dining room. "It adds to the evening," he says, and he's right. I scrape my plate clean—*Scrape!* The veal was superb.

In fact, I'd call the whole experience a masterpiece.

FRED'S BACKSIDE DELI

**501 BEECH MOUNTAIN PKWY., BEECH MOUNTAIN, NC 28604,
(828) 387-4838, FREDSGENERAL.COM**

I love to ski.

I feel completely free when swishing down a slope, utterly away from the worries of the world. Except when headed straight for a giant mogul.

Minus the moguls, I thoroughly enjoy my wintertime trips to Beech Mountain: the crisp air, snowcapped ridges, and great open vastness of it all. I'm a million miles away but just a few hours from home. Time to don the gloves and goggles. But first, breakfast.

Fred's is the place to go. Fred's General Mercantile sits atop Beech as though it *belongs* there, as if Beech wouldn't be Beech without it. It's a country store with an A-frame roof and twinkly lights, the roof red and store blueish, which gives it a worn weathered look but a welcoming one, too, especially when snow blankets the drive and clumps on the bushes and porch rails. Fred's is that toasty escape from the cold, the yellow glow in the blizzard, a Shangri-La on the white-topped hill with piping coffee waiting for chattering teeth.

Beech Mountain is the highest point east of the Mississippi: 5,056 feet up. It's true: The highest point east is south, in North Carolina, where people really do ski and not just on bunny slopes. There are moguls indeed.

And there's Fred's. There's always Fred's, the beacon at Beech, open every day of the year.

I clop my boots on the porch and enter, and the woodsy aroma is comforting, like what I'd smell inside a log cabin. The floor creaks, and the aisles are loaded: shirts, boots, skis, tools, groceries.

"Here we are on top of a mountain, and you can get just about anything you want," says Fred. He has an easy manner, a reddish beard and lumberjack shirt, and I get the feeling he's never been in a hurry. He makes you want to sip that piping coffee and chat a while and hear his story. "Good clean air, a beautiful place," he says in his sleepy southern drawl. "Life is pretty easy here."

In 1970 Fred Pfohl was a student at Appalachian State University in Boone and needed a job. He found one on the ski slopes at Beech and couldn't have been happier—except when he was forced to crawl down the slick, curvy mountain for a loaf of bread and gallon of milk. "There were a lot of things needed up here, and it was three and a half miles to Banner Elk." Years later, on a winter day in '79, he opened Fred's General Mercantile, which included a small cafe.

Fred's Backside Deli is downstairs. Keep an eye out for the sign above the candy rack with the cardboard finger pointing to the steps, which are steep and narrow. Watch your head and bring your appetite.

Scrambled eggs and bacon, grits and biscuits, cinnamon rolls, too. And for lunch: burgers, tuna melts, and Reubens, plus homemade soups and salads. "Not extra fancy," Fred says, "but we specialize in it being extra good."

The setting is as laid back as he is, friendly and warm—though it's mighty cold outside. One wall is lined with windows, and there's nothing but snow beyond the pane, pure and undisturbed.

I find I envy Fred and the life he's built with his wife, Margie, who's upstairs in the store, probably ringing up a winter coat or a sled or just a Snickers bars—no better snack for the slopes. I can't wait to ski. But just another minute in the deli with Fred.

We talk about nothing in particular, and both of us keep turning to the windows. "Snow flurry or two this morning," he says in his sleepy drawl. "But now the Carolina blue sky's beginning to prevail."

He's right, it is, and we sip and watch the sun peek through the clouds.

"Another typical, beautiful, winter day on Beech Mountain," he says.

DOLLY'S DAIRY BAR

128 PISGAH HWY., PISGAH FOREST, NC 28768, (828) 862-6610

There may be more summer camps in Transylvania County than anywhere else in the country—and more ice cream flavors named after summer camps.

Dolly's Dairy Bar sits at the entrance to Pisgah National Forest. "People come out after a long hike, and what better way to end their day than with ice cream," says owner Robert Lee who took over from Dolly when she retired.

Dolly Childers lives up the road and still pops in, often taking a seat in a rocking chair on the front porch. "I love the kids," she says. "It's all about the kids." Long ago, she began naming ice cream flavors after summer camps: Gwynn Valley Gold Rush, Tekoa Brownie

Fixation, Keystone Sunrise, Green Valley Plunge. "Puts a smile on a lot of kids' faces." Indeed, it does.

"Best ice cream place I've ever been to."

"Best in the country."

"I love Dolly's."

I learn one of the most popular flavors is Rockbridge Chocolate Illusion, which includes bits of brownie and pieces of cocoa, mixed with pie crust and dark chocolate ice cream. No illusion at all: chocolatey and good.

Dolly's Dairy Bar is thirty minutes from Asheville and just around the corner from Brevard, a town that's a haven for mountain bikers. And honeymooners.

I meet an older couple at Dolly's sitting on a stone bench near the parking lot and clutching cones like kids. "This is our honeymoon," the man says. "Fifty-seventh anniversary of a honeymoon!" They both laugh so hard they smear their faces and reach for napkins. I wonder if they're eating the flavor called Merrie Wood Boo-Woop, which sounds silly and funny and romantic all in one.

"I came here for the amazing scenery," another camper tells me between licks. "But I didn't realize how amazing the ice cream would be. Amazing," he says and licks again.

FRENCH BROAD CHOCOLATE LOUNGE

10 S. PACK SQUARE, ASHEVILLE, NC 28801, (828) 252-4181, FRENCHBROADCHOCOLATE.COM

I watch a straight line of liquid chocolate flow directly into a white porcelain cup.

It looks like a coffee cup set beneath the open spigot of a coffee brewer, but the brewer dispenses chocolate instead. Thick, rich chocolate.

French Broad Chocolate Lounge is clean and sleek with chromium appliances and shiny countertops, stools and small tables, long windows, sunlight and airiness. Dreaminess. An epiphany.

"She was making truffles as Christmas gifts for her friends and family," Dan Rattigan says of his wife, Jael, and mentions the word *epiphany.*

Jael uses the word *destiny.* "I felt like I found it when my hands were covered in chocolate, and I felt like chocolate was what would bring me happiness."

Jael is dark haired, Dan messy haired, both mid-thirties, hip, and adventurous. But they didn't start that way. He was in law school, she was in business school, both in Minnesota, which is where they met in 2003. And then came Jael's epiphany. Or was it destiny? "And the next day was like, 'Okay, what are we gonna do?'"

They dropped out of school and drove south to Costa Rica, a lengthy drive but with a lengthy vehicle, a forty-foot school bus, which Dan converted to run on vegetable oil. They headed to "a part of Costa Rica that produces cacao," he says and explains that cacao is a key ingredient of chocolate. The journey included another ingredient, too. "Right before we left Minneapolis, we found out we were pregnant with our first son."

Dan and Jael settled in a small seaside Costa Rican village where they opened a cafe and dessert shop called Bread & Chocolate. They lived in an apartment above the shop with their little boy Sam and enjoyed two successful years before realizing they weren't really beach people. So they sold the cafe to one of their cooks and wondered what to do next. Move back to the States? But where?

"And over and over, we kept hearing people say, 'You guys would love Asheville,'" Jael says. They thought about it and followed their instincts and made the move in 2006—pregnant again. "We like to birth babies and businesses together."

Today, their business is in Asheville's Pack Square downtown. "We are fully bean to bar," Dan explains. "All the chocolate we use in house we make from cacao beans we import from countries of origin, including Costa Rica, Nicaragua, and Peru."

He leads me through a door that says, "Chocolate Factory" and into a large industrial-type room humming with machinery. He shows me the cacao beans, which look like peanuts I buy at the ballpark. They're piled on a stainless-steel table where teams sort them by hand. In another section, a woman loosens chocolate balls from a rubbery mold and sets them on trays. "She's de-molding our truffle ganache," Dan says. He also shows me a variety of chocolate bars, all handmade at the Chocolate Lounge.

"How'd you learn to do all this?" I ask.

"We're still learning." And he's clearly excited about it. I can hear the excitement in his voice, the way he explains the process, the different steps, the potential that lies ahead.

"We started a company of two people and have grown it to one of seventy employees," Jael says, "and our challenges have changed a lot."

But I imagine the challenges are part of the adventure. And I get the feeling Dan and Jael love an adventure, and this one seems both rich and fulfilling. Maybe a bit edgy and unpredictable as well, though laced with a bit of—*dreaminess*. Who knows what delicious turn the road might take? Perhaps another *epiphany* awaits.

I watch Jael fill another cup full of chocolate, thick rich chocolate, all the way to the brim. Dan watches, too, and for a moment he turns reflective. "We just have to keep guessing and moving forward with faith that we've got the right idea in mind."

THE COPPER DOOR

**2 SULLIVAN ST., HAYESVILLE, NC 28904, (828) 389-8460,
THECOPPERDOOR.COM**

Fewer than a thousand people live in Hayesville.

Opening a high-end restaurant in such a tiny town must have been crazy. Dennis Barber is crazy busy.

He's owner and chef of The Copper Door, and just four years after opening the door, Open Table listed it as one of the top one hundred restaurants in America—top one hundred out of twelve thousand surveyed. Now that *is* crazy. In Hayesville? Home to just a few hundred people?

The people come from somewhere, because Chef Dennis has steak on the grill, lamb in the oven, and escargot in the pan, multiples of each, with orders for grouper and foie gras in the waiting—multiples

of those, too. But he's not flustered; he sometimes whistles while he works.

He wears his gray hair slicked back and rust-colored uniform buttoned at the top. He stands at a serving counter, eyes bouncing from the cooks at the grill to a display screen at his right. He tracks incoming orders even as his team slides outgoing ones on the shelf, which Dennis inspects and often completes with an accoutrement here, a touch of sauce there. He doesn't labor over the flames nowadays—his cooks are responsible for that—but he oversees the entire arrangement, from designing the menu to ordering the meat. And only the best.

I watch him ladle mushroom bisque into a bowl, which he does artfully, gracefully, creating distance between bowl and spoon as a waiter would between bottle and glass when pouring fine wine. Although the performance reminds me more of a conductor. He lifts the long-handled ladle like a wand rising on a high note—and his aim is true.

He was born in Memphis, grew up in New Orleans, and for nearly a decade was an Air Force B-52 bombardier. It was a thrilling ride, although he'd always wanted to own a restaurant. In time, he stopped flying and started cooking. He enrolled in culinary school and eventually became a certified chef based in New Orleans. In 1988 the Republican National Convention came to town, and Dennis was chosen to cook for President and Mrs. Reagan.

In the 1990s he wound up in Atlanta, out of the food business and bored, when one day he heard about a couple of buildings for sale in Clay County, North Carolina—in Hayesville—one of them an old gas station. "Burned out buildings that needed restoration," he says.

Most people might have walked away, but the mountain scenery held him, and so did Hayesville with its quiet charm: stores and offices with American flags out front, the historic red-brick courthouse at the center of town, peaceful Lake Chatuge rippling at the foot of the Blue Ridge. "I looked around and saw the potential for the area, and I thought, *You know what? Let's give it a whirl.*"

He turned the old gas station into The Copper Door and opened in 2007—the front door is copper, of course, which hints at the elegance to come.

It's dark inside, romantically so. The hostess is young and blonde, pretty in a black dress. She greets guests with a gracious smile and escorts them down a short corridor that opens into the dining area

with walls of bronze-colored wood and a magnificent stone fire-place; the sandy stone lends a certain majesty to the room, as do the crisply set tables draped with white tablecloths and topped with long-stemmed glasses.

"Well, it's so unexpected," a woman in a booth says. She's dining with her husband and two other couples, all in their mid-seventies, I suspect. The woman appears elegant herself in a high-collared dress. She and her husband retired to Hayesville part time, she says, spending summer and fall months in the mountains. "We never expected to find this little jewel in a small town."

"I think it's the best I've ever been to," adds the woman next to her.

"The best restaurant?" I ask. She nods. "In Hayesville?" The whole table nods.

A second dining room adjoins the first, brighter and adorned with colorful artwork. "The Ruby Room," explains the young hostess to a newly seated group. "All the flower paintings you see, they were painted by Chef's mother, and her name was Ruby."

Chef Dennis admits to some art talent himself. At one point he'd been crafting sculptures, creating them out of—copper.

"A beautiful piece," he says, twirling a plate that's just been set on the serving shelf before him. The centerpiece is a filet mignon dripping with butter and topped with a scallop. Seconds later, the cook slides another entrée next to it. "Snowy grouper," Dennis announces and twirls that plate, too; the grouper comes delicately drizzled. "From the Gulf of Mexico. Serving it tonight with a lemon basil sauce."

I admire the presentation of the dishes, along with the temperament of Dennis. I would think a chef of his caliber—with New Orleans roots, having served a US president and First Lady, now operating a sophisticated establishment with a wine list of more than three hundred varieties—might be rather put off by a news team hovering over his filet and grouper, not to mention his grilled salmon and crawfish crepe, but Dennis is laid back, even when the medium rib eye comes out a tad less than medium.

"One of America's top one hundred restaurants?" I ask. He calmly tells the cook to give the rib eye another go and says he's grateful and humbled by the accolades. "But—in Hayesville?" I say. I can't help it; I keep asking the same question.

Chef Dennis turns from the serving shelf and for a moment seems to leave the business of the grill behind him. His eyes appear to focus not on me or the camera but on something else, something distant. Something beyond the copper door.

"I wake up every morning," he says, "and I look at these mountains God created . . ." He lets the sentence hang, as if pausing to look at the mountains he cannot see—yet seeing them just the same.

"Gorgeous," he says at last.

CONCLUSION

SECONDS

We've reached the end.

Did you visit each one? All 101? Bet you have your delectable favorites. I suppose I have my own, although I don't really look at the mom-and-pops that way. Instead, I view them more as one, as a whole, a rich and flavorful fabric of North Carolina. And yet each does have its own colorful distinction, which is what makes the trips so much fun.

I do know there are more good eats out there, beyond the margins of this book, past the shoulders of the interstate, in the town up ahead or around another bend in the road. Many more than 101. I hope to visit them, too. What a delicious state to explore!

But for now, you've come to the conclusion, the final page, end of the list—but never the end of the road. Thanks for keeping the book on the seat beside you. Or has it been in the glove box by the owner's manual? Or in the trunk next to the spare? Well, anyway, you're still reading, holding so many treasured restaurants in your hands, 101 down-home classics at your fingertips. Who says you can't turn another page? Flip back to the beginning? Do it all over again?

Can I come, too? I'm always up for seconds.

INDEX

ABOUT THE AUTHOR

Scott Mason has been a television reporter for more than 35 years and WRAL's Tar Heel Traveler since 2007. His more than 100 journalism awards include 20 regional Emmys and three National Edward R. Murrow awards, one of broadcasting's highest honors. He has twice been named North Carolina Television Reporter of the Year. He lives in Raleigh, North Carolina.

For more information about Scott Mason and his books go to: TheTarHeelTraveler.com, smason@wral.com.